The Ridiculously Simple Guide to Pixel Go, PixelBook and Pixel Slate

GETTING STARTED WITH CHROME OS

Scott La Counte

RIDICULOUSLY
SIMPLE BOOKS

ANAHEIM, CALIFORNIA

www.RidiculouslySimpleBooks.com

Table of Contents

Disclaimer: *Please note, while every effort has been made to ensure accuracy, this book is not endorsed by Google and should be considered unofficial.*

INTRODUCTION

A laptop less than $300? That used to be unthinkable! Even more unthinkable was a computer that relied on an operating system that wasn't Windows, Linux, or Mac.

In 2011, Google disrupted the computer industry when it introduced the Chromebook. The lightweight computers with small price tags were the perfect solution for schools already using Google's suite of free cloud-based tools (Docs, Sheets, Slides, etc.).

To the average professional, Chromebooks have been more of a novelty best suited for casual use. In 2013, Google tried to change this with the Chromebook Pixel—its first higher-end Chromebook. While most saw it as a worthy first effort, it was not largely viewed as ready for primetime.

Google discontinued the Chromebook Pixel in 2017 and announced its successor in October of 2017: The Pixelbook. Everything about the successor proved that Google had learned from previous generation Chromebooks and was ready to seriously compete with the Windows Surface and MacBook.

The hardware alone matched high-end Mac and Windows computers, but the software is where the Pixelbook really shines. In addition to Google Assistant, a Siri-like tool for productivity, the computer also is amongst the first Chromebooks to be able to run Android apps—combined with a convertible touchscreen, this means you can leave your tablet at home. For a better comparison of how the computer ranks against Windows and Mac, see Appendix A.

Still, there was a void to be filled. The Pixelbook was so high-end that most apps could never meet its potential. Google needed a good laptop—but most critics said they needed one without all the bells and whistles, and at a cheaper price. Google answered in 2019 with the Pixel Go. A Chromebook that feels high-end but comes at nearly half the price of the Pixelbook.

If you've used any computer then the Pixel Go, Pixelbook, and even Slate will be easy enough to use as soon as you open it up for the first time. If you really want to take advantage of all the features and be as productive as possible, then this guide will help. Almost everything in this book will also apply to other Chromebooks.

Let's get started!

[1]

Tell Me the Basics and Keep It Ridiculously Simple

This chapter will cover:

- What's Chrome OS
- Pixelbook vs. Slate
- The Device(s)
- The Keyboard
- The Trackpad

A WORD (OR PARAGRAPH OR TWO) ABOUT CHROME OS

For years, Google has taken what you could call the "Apple approach" to computers and tablets. Computers ran Chrome and tablets ran Android (e.g. iPads run iOS and MacBooks run MacOS). Like iPads and MacBooks, there were similarities between Android tablets and Chrome computers. But there were also differences.

The Pixel Slate breaks this tradition by running the same operating system (OS) that you are familiar with if you have a Chromebook. What's more, newer Chromebooks can also download Android apps. That means if there's an app you love on your phone, you can use it on your computer as well.

Pixelbook vs. Slate

In 2018, a lot of people were expecting a new Pixelbook to be announced; in its place, however, was a powerful tablet that is cheaper than the Pixelbook (but more expensive than the Pixel Go). It begs the question: should you ditched the traditional laptop and replaced it with a tablet? Not exactly.

There is a place for both devices.

Both are crafted from aluminum and feature tough Gorilla Glass; this makes them feel like they're worth the price. Unlike some Chrome tablets and laptops that feel like they're nothing but cheap plastic that will crack any minute, both these tablets are light but durable.

The Pixel Go is made out of magnesium; the material is cheaper, but it doesn't feel like the cheap plastic of some laptops. There's also a rigid bottom that's meant to make it easier to grip and carry.

In terms of performance, the Pixelbook is running an Intel processor that's a year old, but it's still faster than the base Pixel Slate. Does it matter? If this was a normal OS, then absolutely! What you have to realize with Chrome OS is you don't need a lot of power to use it. The Pixel go is running a Core m3, which is technically slower than the Pixelbook, but you won't notice the performance on most apps.

The screens are both 12.3 inches and have dual speakers; the Slate's screen is sharper at 293 pixels over the Pixelbooks 235. The Pixel Go is 13.3 inches with 166 ppi.

Both devices have USB-C ports (more on that later), so if you need to add photos via an SD card, then you'll need and adaptor.

The Slate is about a pound lighter than the Pixelbook and Pixel Go, and also slimmer. When you add on the optional keyboard accessory to the

Slate, however, they become almost identical in both size and weight.

If you are considering which one to purchase, you won't go wrong with either device. It really comes down to preference and what you are using it for. If you want something that is more traditional, yet still has the option of becoming a tablet by folding it back, then the Pixelbook is for you. If you are looking for something a little cheaper and lighter, and like using tablets, then the Slate is the obvious choice. The Pixel Go is the most economical of the three, but still an excellent computer with battery life that surpasses the Pixelbook. One of the biggest drawbacks is the screen doesn't fold back, so you can't use it like a tablet. Just remember: the Slate is bigger than most tablets. It's a good idea to see one up close before buying.

The Device

The Pixelbook, Pixel Go, and Pixel Slate are all obviously thin machines. That means it may be lacking some of the traditional ports that you are used to—notably traditional USB.

Two of the inputs—one on the right and one on the left on the Pixelbook and Pixel Go—are USB-C. If you have a newer Android phone, then you probably are already familiar with USB-C. It's the newest

USB standard, and it's much faster than the traditional USB ports. Adaptors for USB-C input ports are very cheap to purchase online. A few I recommend picking up:

SanDisk makes a very inexpensive (32GB for under $20) Dual USB drive; this small USB stick makes it possible to switch quickly between traditional USB and USB-C. So, you can save data off an older computer and open it on your Pixelbook.

Pixelbook can be wirelessly displayed on your TV using devices like Chromecast. If you don't mind wires, a USB-C to HDMI adaptor is a smoother option. Adaptors cost between $10 and $20 online.

With only two USB-C input ports, you might run out of space quickly. If you have multiple things you need to plug in, then pick up a USB-C hub. You can find them for under $20 online. These hubs let you plug in multiple USB devices (more expensive models also have input for SD cards and HDMI).

The Pixelbook has a long-lasting 10-hour battery; the Pixel Go will last two hours longer. That will work fine for most people. For power users or people who travel often, a USB-C battery pack can be purchased for $50 to $100. Most of these chargers can also simultaneously charge your phone and other devices.

Personally, I don't use the Google Pixelbook Pen; for most users, it's an expensive add-on that you most likely will never use. It is a good option, however, for artist or those that require the highest accuracy with the touch display.

Remember that the power adaptor for both devices is also USB-C; this means that if you need to charge your computer or tablet, then you will only have one extra port left.

The second input type (located on the left side of the computer) is for sound.

Finally, the two buttons (both on the left side of the computer) are for volume and power. Holding the power button will send the computer to the login screen; if you continue to hold it, the computer will power off.

The Keyboard

(this applies to the Pixelbook and Pixel Go, but will also work on the optional Pixel Slate Keyboard)

The layout of the keyboard isn't completely different from other computers, but there are a few keys you might not be familiar with. The list below is an overview of those keys.

	Searches all the apps installed on your computer as well as the

	web. This button is where the Caps Lock key normally is—to use Caps Lock, hit this button and the Alt at the same time.
	Launches the Google Assistant (Google's version of Siri).
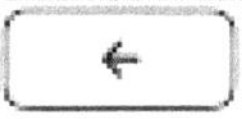	Goes to the previous page in your browser history.
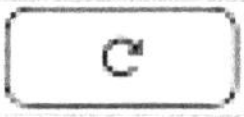	Reloads your current page.
	This puts your current application in full screen mode; all the tabs and the launcher will be hidden.
	Shows all windows in Overview mode.
	Dims the screen (F5).
	Make the screen brighter (F6).
	Play/pause (F7).
	Mute (F8).
	Lower the volume (F9).
	Raise the volume (F10).
	Open your status area (where your account picture appears).

The Trackpad (Pixelbook feature)

Trackpad's have come a long way over the years; the left / right buttons are technically gone, for instance, but they are still there in theory. Google has implemented a series of gestures to perform all of the essential mouse-type functions. You'll be using the trackpad in the following five ways:

Moving the Cursor – this is the standard mouse pointing action. Just move one finger across the trackpad in whichever direction you'd like to move the cursor.

Left-click – pressing down anywhere on the lower half of the trackpad will perform a left-click. You can also tap anywhere along the trackpad to left-click, but this must be enabled in the settings, which we'll discuss a little later.

Right-click – right-clicking is done by clicking (or tapping) the trackpad with two fingers instead of one. This is often used for bringing up context menus.

Scrolling – in place of a traditional mouse's scroll-wheel, placing two fingers on the trackpad and moving them simultaneously up / down or left / right will scroll whatever item you're looking at. This comes in handy for nearly everything—web pages, documents, etc.

Dragging and Dropping – this is probably the most complicated trackpad gesture of the bunch, useful for moving items to and from Google Drive or other locations on your hard drive. To perform this gesture, click on an item with one finger while simultaneously moving it with a second finger. When you've got the item moved to where you'd like it, let go by removing both fingers from the trackpad. It might take you a little bit of practice to get the hang of this one.

[2] All About Chrome OS

This chapter will cover:

- User Accounts
- Settings Overview

Chrome OS (the browser on all Pixels) is a very close relative of Google's Internet browser, Google Chrome. As the owner of a Chromebook, you'll quickly see that Chrome is about to become a very big part of your life. This is a good thing; it's a fast, easy-to-use web browser with all kinds of features and seemingly unlimited potential for enhancement thanks to apps and extensions available in the Chrome Web Store. The Chrome browser means so much more than just web browsing in Chrome OS though, due to the fact that almost every app you run in Chrome OS runs inside a Chrome browser window. Don't worry if that sounds bizarre at first—you'll get the hang of it quickly and I'll walk you through everything you need to know!

The Chrome Web Store contains products that are similar enough to major desktop applications that you'll hardly be able to tell the difference. As a bonus, many of them are completely free (and if you've ever shelled out for Photoshop, I know that's going to come as a relief!).

Since most of Chromebook's functionality happens within a browser, Chromebook users can get to the majority of their Chromebook work from any computer with the free Google Chrome browser installed. Google's cloud storage system—Google Drive—is baked into Chrome OS and steadily saves your work as you go. As long as you're connected to Wi-Fi, if catastrophe strikes your physical Chromebook, your important files and documents are safe and sound in the cloud.

If you're scratching your head at this point, don't worry. Chromebook is easy to use, and the best way to understand it is to turn the thing on, roll up your sleeves, and dive right in. And we're going to do just that in the next chapter!

USER ACCOUNTS

One of the best features about any Chromebook is the ability to add user accounts; unlike other computers, you can take all of your settings with you. So let's say you have a Chromebook, and log in to another Chromebook. All of your apps, settings, customizations are there waiting for you. It's almost like you are using your personal computer even though you are logged in as a guest. This also means when you get another computer in the future, it's very simple to set up. Just log in and you are done!

Having multiple accounts also makes it very easy to share a computer in your household. From the login screen, you can either add a user or log in as a guest. Anyone who has a Google account (if you have Gmail then you have one—if you don't have Gmail you might have one without knowing it, as this is what many businesses use), can set up an account on your computer. Don't worry: this won't give other users access to any of your files or personal settings.

There is only one important thing to remember with regard to user accounts: set up the device owner first! If you use another account to sign into the computer for the first time, then that's the device owner and the person who will have administrator rights that other users won't have. There's no way to transfer ownership to another user, so you would have to reset your computer if that happens.

SETTINGS OVERVIEW

We'll discuss the settings a little further throughout this book, but there are a few settings you'll want to know about right now.

User Accounts

If you want to disable people from being able to log in to your settings, then log in to your account, click on your user profile image (bottom right corner of the screen), then click the settings button:

From here, you'll be taken to a browser window with a list of some of the most common settings. Scroll to the bottom of the list and click the button labeled "Manage Other Users." By default, everything is toggled on; click it once to toggle it off. Hit the back button and it saves your settings automatically.

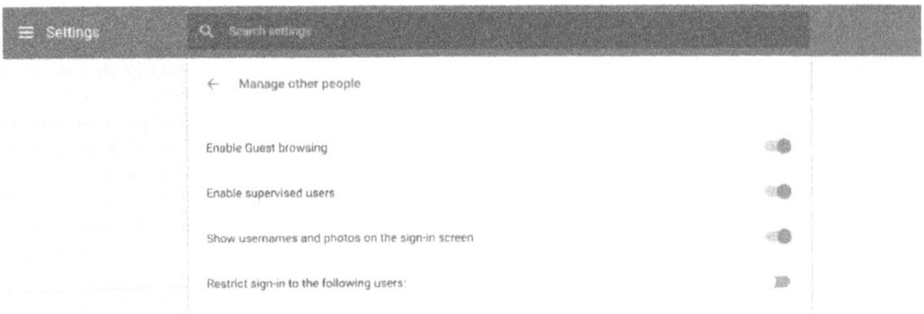

Keyboard Settings

The location of the Alt key on a computer keyboard is what a Mac user might use as the Command key. There are several keys like this. You can either retrain your mind or you can go into the keyboard settings and change the shortcuts around a little. In the settings you can also change things like the language.

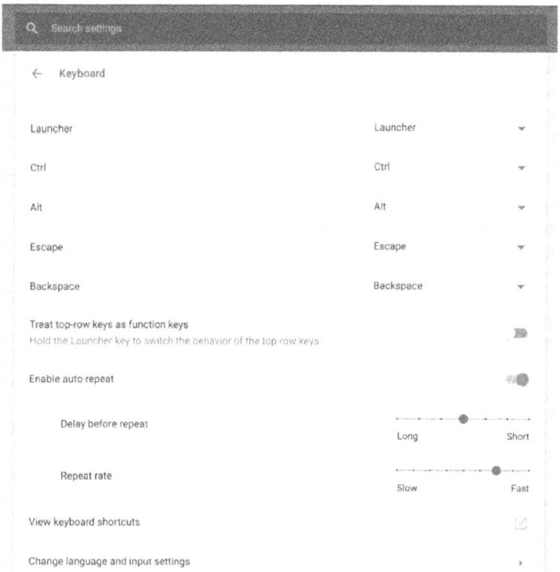

Touchpad Settings

Mac users will be a little annoyed with scrolling on their new computer! That's because the scrolling on an Apple device is the opposite of scrolling on the Chromebook! Again, you can either retrain your mind or you can just change the setting. "Australian" is the scrolling you will want. Another setting you will probably want to change is the Touchpad speed; to some users, it might feel a little laggy. It's an easy fix. Just slide the Touchpad speed button to the right for a faster scroll.

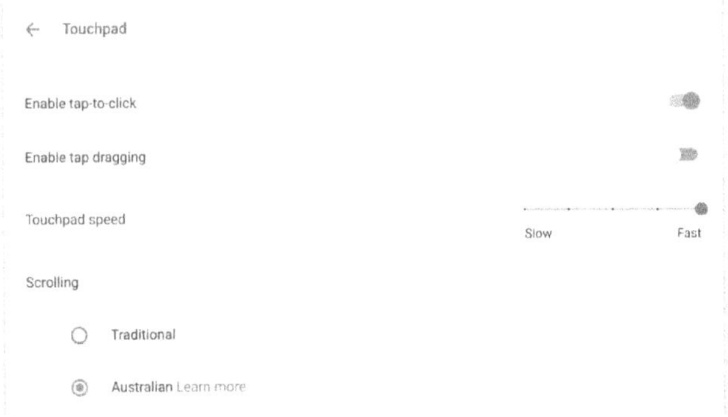

VIRTUAL DESKS

Multitasking on the Pixel isn't anything too new, but Chrome OS 78 introduced some expanded features for virtual desktops.

What is Virtual Desks? It's basically having different workspaces open. You could have one desktop for work and one for personal use, for example.

To use it, press the button on the top row that looks like a square with two lines.

That opens up your current desk (or, as in the example below, nothing is open).

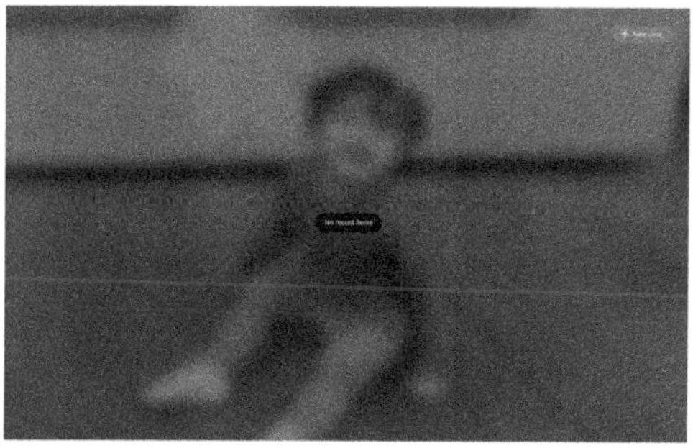

To open a new desk (or desktop) just tap the +New desk button in the upper right corner. You'll immediately see a thumbnail for the desktops and you can toggle between them.

[3] GETTING AROUND THE OS

This chapter will cover:

- The Desktop
- Launcher and Chrome Shelf
- Chrome Windows
- Files and Google Drive
- Offline Mode

Google's OS seems much like a marriage between Windows OS and Mac OS, and that's a good thing, because with very little instruction, everything will start feeling natural. In this section, you'll get a crash course in the basic features of the OS and where things are located.

DESKTOP

Your desktop takes up the bulk of the screen. It includes a desktop wallpaper image, which can be customized, and you can also store files and shortcuts here for easy access, just like other desktops. Chances are, however, you'll probably find yourself not making much use of the desktop space. Chrome's intuitive interface makes it easier just to store everything in your Google Drive. I've used Chrome OS for many years, and I find the desktop is usually just a place to put a pretty picture.

THE LAUNCHER AND CHROME SHELF

The Launcher button is similar to the Start button on a Windows computer—only a bit simpler. Clicking on the Launcher button will reveal every app associated with your Google account. This apps menu does extend to the right, and you may need to use the horizontal page indicator icons at the bottom of the menu to move from screen to screen.

Next to the Apps button, you'll find your Chrome "shelf." You might be used to thinking of this area as a taskbar or dock, but in Chrome, it's called the shelf. The shelf contains shortcuts to your favorite apps and documents, and lets you know what's currently running. In the screenshot above, you can see that I'm currently running the Chrome browser, Gmail, the app HipChat, and the Files app, due to the small gray dot under those icons.

To the far right (where your photo is) is the Systems Tray Menu; this is where you'll see settings, apps that have updated, and battery life.

CHROME WINDOWS

Chrome is almost entirely browser-based; there are a few more traditional looking apps (like Google Hangouts), but most of the apps you see on your Chrome shelf are more like shortcuts to a web page. I'll explain the apps that come with the Chromebook and how to get additional ones later in this book.

FILES AND GOOGLE DRIVE

Every computer has "local" storage—which is all the stuff (files, photos, documents) that are stored directly on the computer; Windows computers have File/System Explorer; Mac computers have Finder; and Chrome computers have Files. Chrome computers have one extra storage drive: Google Drive. Google Drive is cloud-based, which means whatever you store there will be available on the Internet (privately, unless you make it public). This makes it easy to store a file that you want to use on another computer. The Files app shows you both local files (on your computer) and cloud files (stored online). If you were to connect a USB storage device like a flash drive or an external hard drive, you'd see that in Files as well.

Keep in mind that Google Drive is not unlimited storage; your Google account has 15GB of free storage. After that, it's $1.99 a month and up. It's a very inexpensive solution, and one you should consider for backing up files you store on your computer. Also, buying any new Chromebook may mean you are qualified for free storage. You can see Google's current offerings here: https://www.google.com/chromebook/offers/

OFFLINE

The Chromebook is designed to be used online. That said, the Internet is not required. Even Google's suite of online apps (Docs, Sheets, and Slides) can be used offline. If you plan to work on a Google Doc file (or Sheets/Slides) make sure you move it into the offline folder before logging off.

[4]

All About Chrome Browser

This chapter will cover:

- Anatomy of the Chrome Window
- Tabs and Windows
- Incognito
- Bookmarks
- History
- Passwords
- Autofill
- Chrome Extensions
- Web Store and Apps

- Installing and Managing Chrome Content

THE CHROME BROWSER

The web browser that comes standard with your Chromebook is, for all intents and purposes, the very same version of Chrome that's available for Windows, OSX, and Linux computers. So if you're already using Chrome on another device, then there's very little learning curve. One thing you'll love right away is all of your bookmarks and settings will be carried over from one device to the next. There are still a few things you'll want to know about, so I'll cover them here.

You'll notice that opening Chrome doesn't automatically put the browser into full screen mode. You can resize the Chrome window two different ways—by pressing the green maximize button or by tapping the three dots in the top right corner and then tapping the full screen button next to the zoom options.

If you're using Chrome on other devices, you'll be able to access all of your currently open pages and bookmarks by clicking Other Devices, (click the three dots, hover over history, and scroll to the bottom of the list). If you've accidentally closed a web page, Chrome will save it for a period of time under the Recently Closed menu.

ANATOMY OF A GOOGLE CHROME WINDOW

Chrome stays out of your way, for the most part. The vast majority of a Chrome window is reserved for content—whether it's a web page, a Google Docs document, a game, or any other Chrome app.

Everything you need to manage a Chrome window is located at the top of the page. At the top right corner, you'll see the Back, Forward and Refresh buttons. These are used to navigate back or forward through your recent screen views and to reload a page. They match up with the three keys on the keyboard directly to the right of the ESC key on the top row.

In the center of the top part of the screen, you'll see the address / search bar, known as the Chrome "omnibox." Type a website's address (google.com, facebook.com) here to go directly to that site. You can also use this area as a search bar ("kittens," "DIY birdhouse," etc.).

At the right end of the omnibox, you'll see a star. Click that star to bookmark the web page (I'll go into more detail on this process in just a second).

Finally, at the far top right corner, you'll see the Chrome menu button. Here you'll find everything else you need to manage a Chrome window. I'll refer to this button pretty often throughout this guide!

TABS AND WINDOWS

There are two viewing units to be aware of in Chrome—tabs and windows. Tabs open inside one window, as pictured below. You can open a new tab by pressing CTRL+T (remember: t for tab), by right-clicking the Chrome icon in the shelf, or by clicking 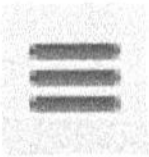 > New Tab.

Opening a page in a new window, on the other hand, opens a completely separate frame (which can then be populated with a new group of tabs, if you like). You can open new windows by pressing CTRL+N (N for new), by right-clicking the Chrome icon on the shelf, or by clicking  > New Window.

When tabs were first introduced, they streamlined the laborious process of switching between several windows while browsing the Internet. As a result, many users now associate tabs with easier workflow. However, on a Chromebook, it's often easier to switch between windows than between tabs, thanks to the Window Switch key on the top row. Pressing the Window Switch key reveals every open window, giving you the title and a visual preview of each one. Keep this in mind when you're formulating your workflow windows / tabs strategy!

BROWSING INCOGNITO

If you're shopping for birthday presents, or doing anything else that you don't want enshrined in your search history, Incognito is the browsing mode for you. Pages you view while in an Incognito tab won't be saved in your history. Search terms won't resurface in your search history, and website cookies won't be stored on your computer. However, if you download or bookmark anything, remember that it will be retained on your system.

To open an Incognito tab in Chrome, press CTRL+SHIFT+N, right-click the Chrome icon on the shelf, or click  > New Window. You can tell at a glance which windows are Incognito by looking for the shadowy figure in sunglasses peeking from behind the top left corner.

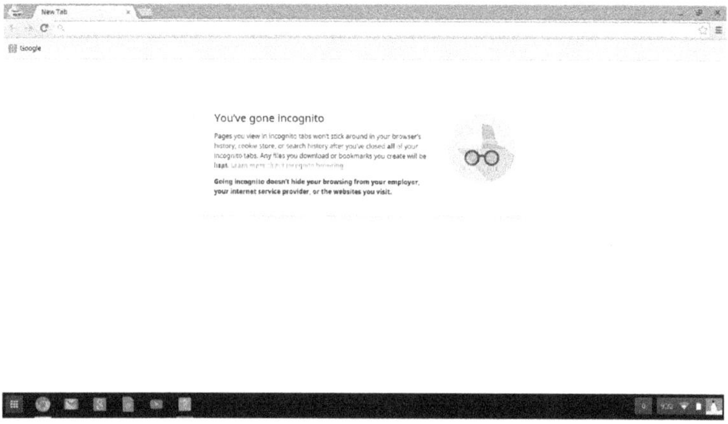

BOOKMARKS

Bookmarks are a handy way to organize your favorite sites for fast access later on. There are a few different ways to bookmark a site. You can click the Star outline in the omnibox, as previously discussed, or you can press CTRL+D. You can also navigate to  > Bookmarks > Bookmark this page.

By default, your bookmarks are stored in the bookmarks bar, which is not visible by default. The bookmarks bar, when enabled, appears underneath the omnibox. To display the bookmarks bar, click  > Bookmarks > Show bookmarks bar, or press

CTRL+SHIFT+B. To hide it, follow the same path or use the same keyboard shortcut.

If you don't like the automatic wording for each bookmark, you can easily edit it, either when adding the bookmark or later by managing your bookmarks. To manage bookmarks, right-click the bookmark and then click Edit (or Delete, or whatever you need to do). Then click  > Bookmarks > Bookmark Manager, or press CTRL+SHIFT+O. Inside the bookmark manager, you can right-click bookmarks to edit them, as pictured below. You can also rearrange the order of your bookmarks either in the Bookmark Manager or by dragging them around on the bookmarks bar itself. The most common edit I make for bookmarks is shortening the name in order to fit as many as possible in my bookmarks bar!

Of course, you may eventually run out of room in the bookmarks bar. If this happens, a double arrow will appear at the end of the bookmarks bar. Clicking the arrow will reveal the rest of your bookmarks. This may be enough for you, but if you'd like a better way of managing large numbers of bookmarks, I recommend organizing your bookmarks into folders. To do this, open the Bookmark Manager (CTRL+SHIFT+O). Click the Folders heading on the left, and then click Add folder.

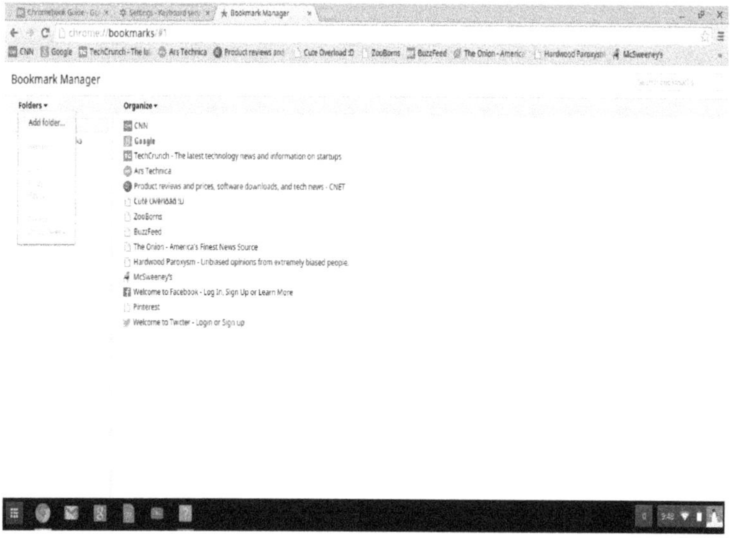

You can add as many folders as you like. Once the folders are added, you can drag your bookmarks into them in the Bookmarks Manager. You can either display your folders on the bookmarks bar or organize them in the Other Bookmarks folder, which you can get to at  > Bookmarks.

Don't forget that in Chrome OS, practically everything you look at is going to be a web page. This means that you can set up bookmarks for Google Docs documents, Google Slides presentations, games, etc. It's a great way to organize a project as well as a way to organize your favorite websites.

RECENT AND HISTORY

Chrome stores your recently viewed pages and full browsing history to make it easy to get back to places you've already been. You can see your recently closed tabs at  > Recent. This is a lifesaver if you accidentally close a tab!

You'll find your full browsing history at  > History or by pressing CTRL+H (H for history). To clear your history at any time, visit your History and then click Clear browsing data. You can either delete history from the past hour, day, week, month, or, as Google so poetically phrases it, the beginning of time. You can also specify what kind of history you want to delete. For example, you can delete your list of recently visited sites, but retain any passwords you've saved in Chrome.

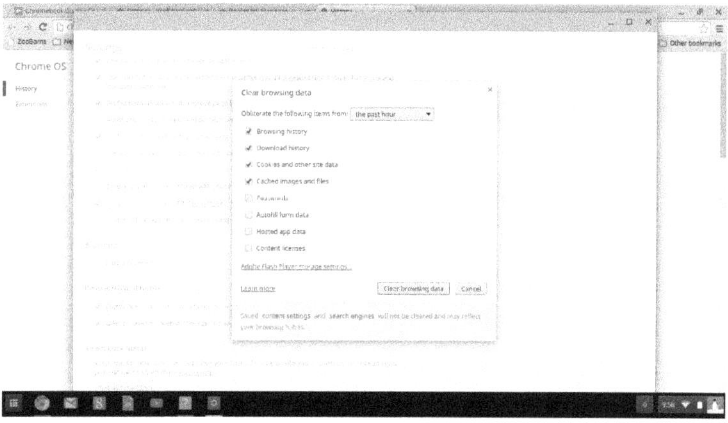

GOOGLE CHROME AND YOUR GOOGLE ACCOUNT

When you set up a new Chromebook, your system will automatically sign you in to the Google Chrome browser. You can sign into Chrome from other computers as well, though. Signing into Chrome will allow you to see your browsing history from other Chrome sessions on other computers, your stored passwords, your extensions, and more. To sign into Chrome, click Sign in at the top right corner of a Chrome browser window.

STORED PASSWORDS

Google Chrome will offer to remember passwords for you whenever you enter them into a website. A popup box will ask you if you want to save the password. You can say Nope to dismiss the box once, or you can click the arrow next to Nope for the Never for this site option.

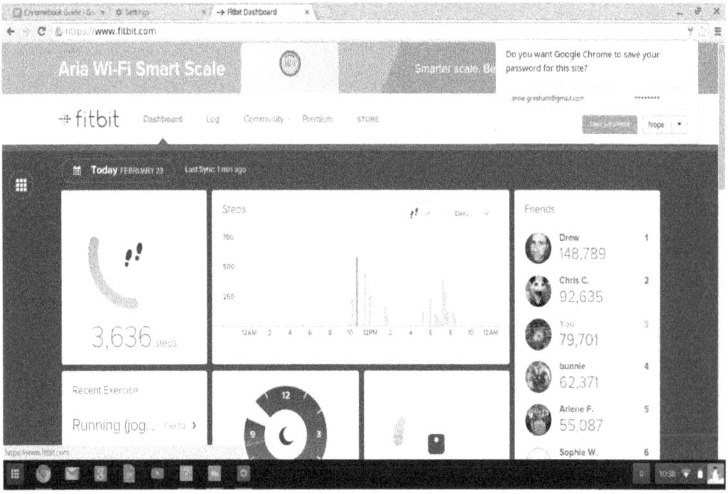

Any passwords you save on your Chromebook or Slate will actually be associated with your Google account. This means that you can use them any time you sign into Chrome, on any computer (though I recommend avoiding signing in on public computers, just to be safe).

If you need to manage your stored passwords, visit  > Settings. At the bottom of the Settings screen, click Show advanced settings. Scroll down until you see the Passwords and Forms heading. Underneath it, click Manage passwords. Here, you can edit or delete your stored passwords. You can also deselect Offer to save your web passwords if you don't want Chrome to store any passwords for you.

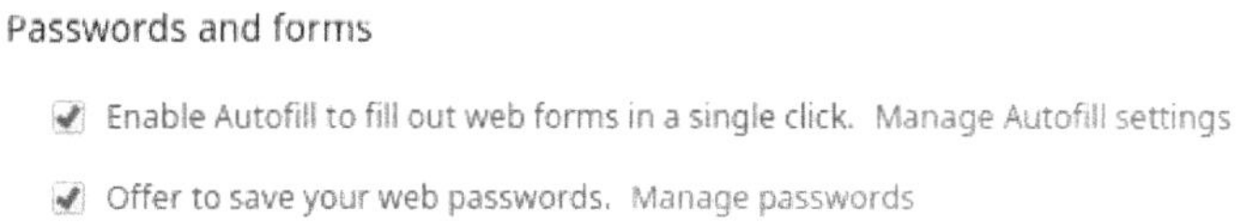

FORM AUTOFILL

Form Autofill handles forms that you repeatedly fill in. It can remember your name, address, phone number, email address, etc. It's useful for repeated data entry, but you may occasionally need to manage your Autofill settings if you move or change your phone number. To do so, visit Settings > Passwords and forms and click Manage Autofill settings.

SEND THIS PAGE

One of the difficulties with Chrome OS is sharing pages with other devices; this is a lot easier with "Send This Page." When you click the address bar, you will notice that there is an icon with a computer and phone; that's the Send This Page icon.

When you tap that, a drop down appears with available devices. Once you click the device, a notification appears on that device that lets you open the page that you just shared.

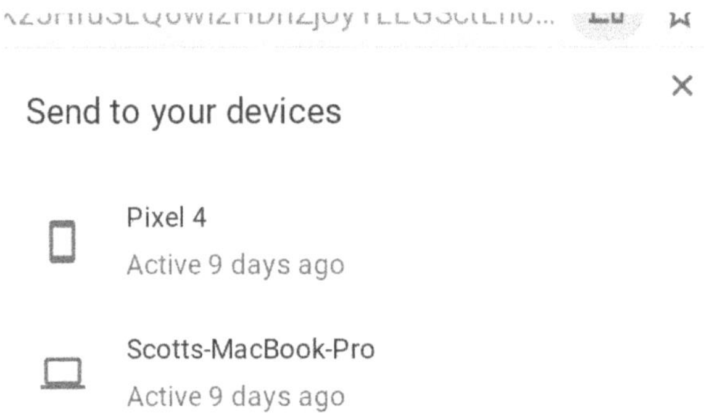

CHROME EXTENSIONS

Extensions extend Chrome's functionality in all kinds of ways, and the enormous range of free extensions to choose from is a huge part of what makes Google Chrome so great. I'll share some of my favorites later in in the book, and you can explore on your own in the Web Store, which I'll cover next.

THE CHROME WEB STORE

You'll want to get to know the Web Store sooner rather than later, since it's where you'll find new apps and extensions for your Chromebook. Fortunately, this "Store" has an enormous free section in it, so tricking out your Chromebook won't necessarily break the bank!

You'll find the Web Store by clicking the Apps button in the lower left corner. If you're an Android user, be aware that the Chrome Web Store isn't exactly the same thing as the Google Play Store, though there's a lot of duplicated content.

There are three big categories in the Store—apps, extensions, and themes. You can choose which broad category you're interested in at the top of the Web Store navigation panel on the left.

Before jumping in, it's worth noting here a very big feature added to both the Chromebook and all new Chromebooks: The Android store!

Why is that important? All those apps that you've already downloaded on your Android tablet or phone can now be downloaded on your computer. It also turns your Chromebook into a tablet. You can download any app from the Play Store and it will install on your computer (play.google.com).

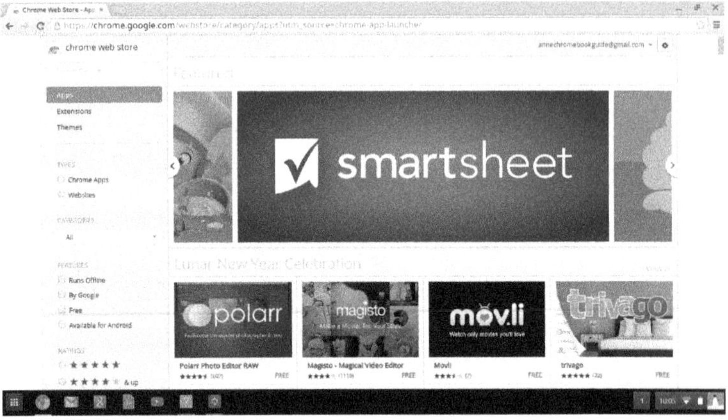

APPS

The apps section of the store contains two types of apps—Chrome apps and website apps. Website "apps" are basically bookmarks. These are websites that you can visit anywhere from any computer, generally with any browser. They're usually free. Chrome apps, on the other hand, make modifications to your Chrome browser in order to function. You will need to be running Chrome in order to use them, and they will need to be installed on the copy of Chrome you're using. This distinction is largely academic for most users. Whether an app is a web app or a Chrome app, adding it to your Chromebook will mean that it appears in your Apps button menu and that it can be pinned to your shelf.

Store apps can be browsed by category, using the dropdown menu under Categories in the left menu. You can also search by feature, like "runs offline" (meaning that the app doesn't require an Internet connection to function), by Google, Free, and Available for Android (very useful if you want to keep your Chromebook and Android smartphone or tablet closely in sync). Finally, you can also sort by the average star rating.

EXTENSIONS

Unlike apps, extensions allow you to do more with every page you visit in Chrome. Extensions let you do more with the Chrome browser, and there are all kinds of possibilities out there. There are extensions that convert currency on web pages for you, help you pin images to your Pinterest boards, generate secure passwords, or help you manage your online privacy.

Like apps, extensions can be narrowed down by category, special features (including Free), and star rating.

THEMES

Themes are similar to desktop wallpapers, but instead of decorating your desktop, they decorate the Chrome window itself. Themes change the appearance of an empty window, typically by showing an image or pattern, and altering the color of the outer edges of the window. In the example below, I've enabled a dark theme.

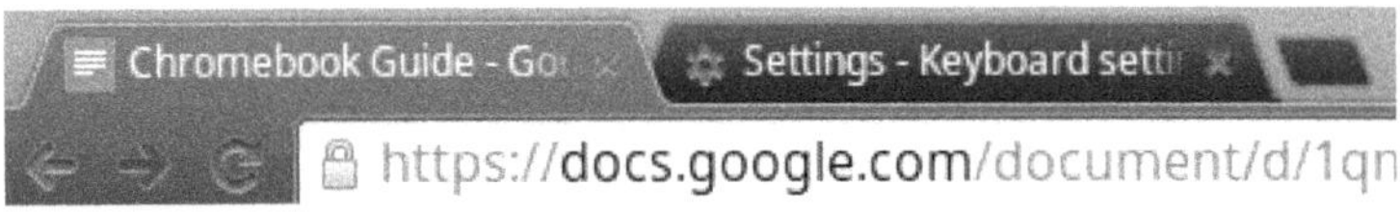

I freely admit that while apps and extensions make me salivate, I'm not quite as enamored with Chrome theming. I'm usually in too much of a hurry to get to my websites, content, and apps to appreciate them. Your mileage may vary, though, and it's not a bad idea to browse some of the free themes in the Store to see if any strike your fancy.

INSTALLING NEW CHROME CONTENT

Installing a new app, extension, or theme is incredibly simple, especially if it's free. To install free content, simply click the FREE text from a search result, and then click the Add to Chrome button that appears on the content's information screen.

If an app, extension, or theme costs money, click the Buy for… button.

Then click Add. At this point, if you haven't already set up Google Wallet, you'll be prompted to do so. Google Wallet is simply Google's credit card manager. Add a payment method as prompted, and Google will save that information for later. You can add more than one payment method if you prefer. From there, confirm the purchase, and your new paid app, extension, or theme will be installed for you.

MANAGING APPS, EXTENSIONS AND THEMES

After you've started amassing a library of apps, extensions and themes, you may occasionally need to temporarily disable or delete them. You can manage your apps by clicking the Apps button and then right-clicking the app you'd like to delete or alter.

Extensions are a little more complicated. You can find your extensions under  > More Tools > Extensions, or under  > History (alternately, press CTRL+H). On the History screen, click Extensions on the left. This will display a list of every installed extension on your system.

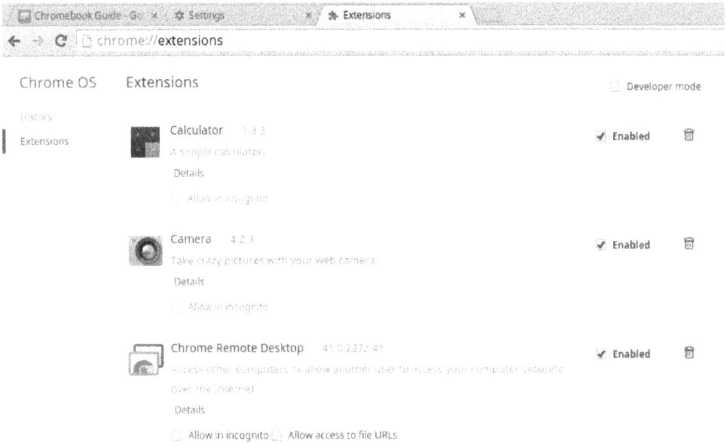

Note that you can disable extensions by deselecting the Enabled checkbox (a good temporary measure), or you can click the trashcan icon to permanently delete something.

[5]

There's a Pre-Installed App for That

This chapter will cover:

- Google Docs, Sheets, Slides
- Scratchpad
- Google+ Hangouts
- Gmail
- YouTube
- Calculator
- Camera
- Chrome Remote Desktop
- Photos

- Keep
- Google Maps and Google My Maps
- Google Forms
- Drawings
- Play Music, Play Books, and Play Movies
- Google Calendar
- Google Play

Just like any computer, your Chromebook will have apps installed right out of the box. Here is an overview and what they're good for.

GOOGLE DOCS

Google Docs, briefly, is Google's version of Microsoft Word or Apple Pages. You can edit a document just like you would in any other processor, but it's all online and synced automatically, which means it's very difficult to lose anything. You can also share documents and collaborate in real time.

Docs really shines through its connection to Google Drive. Anything you start in Google Docs is automatically saved in your Google Drive account—no need to worry about losing work through power failures, device catastrophes, or really just about any other scenario. Changes are saved as you go, and so are versions, so it's easy to revert to an earlier stage of a draft if you need to.

The main Docs menu consists of File, Edit, Insert, Format, Tools, Table, Add-ons, and Help. Each of these menu items contains a dropdown menu full of features. The full power of Docs is beyond the scope of this guide, but we'll show you some of the basics.

Starting a New Google Doc

To start a new document, simply open Docs for the first time, or click File > New to open a new document. Notice that Google Docs > File > New will also let you start new Sheets, Slides, Drawings, or Forms projects as well.

Saving a Google Doc

Google Docs saves everything as you go, so you'll rarely need to save manually. You can find the status of your file to the right of the menu if you're concerned. Google Docs does save your work offline as well, so if you're not connected to Drive, you won't lose your work and you can verify that Chromebook has saved it for you.

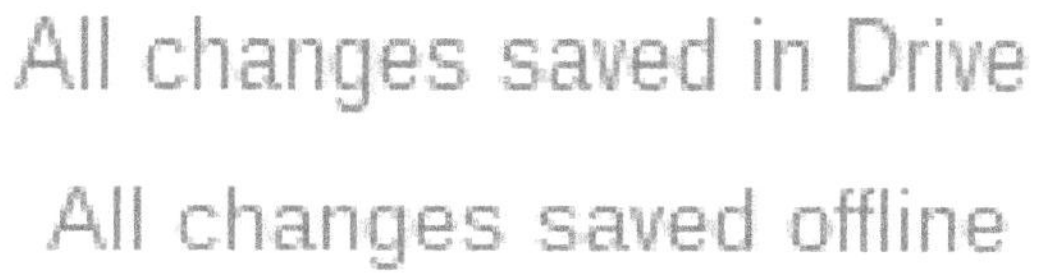

Formatting a Google Doc

You'll find all the standard text editing options you'd expect in the top menu area, including font size, typeface, bold, italic, underline, text color, hyperlinks, and text alignment. If that doesn't cover you, though, you'll also find spacing, lists, indent control, and format clearing under More.

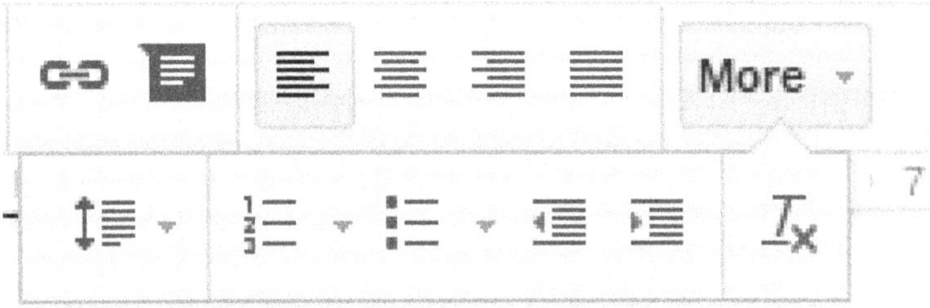

Collaborating Using Google Docs

Google Docs is hands-down one of the easiest ways to work on a group document. To invite people to share your Doc, click the blue Share button in the top right corner (note that hovering over this button will also give you the current shared status of your Doc).

You can add existing Google contacts by entering their names, or you can invite anyone through their email address. Note that your collaborators will need to set up a free Google account to use Google Drive. You can choose the level of access you want collaborators to have—they can edit, comment, or merely view your shared document.

You can remove them at any time by using the Share button again.

When two or more people are editing a document at the same time, you'll be able to see that person's cursor position and watch edits in real time. If you're concerned about losing work, remember that Google Docs saves version history for you, so it's easy to revert if you need to. Click File > See revision history (or press CTRL+ALT+SHIFT+G). By default, revisions are shown grouped into daily periods, but if you want to see changes made by the minute, click Show more detailed revisions at the bottom of the revisions panel. You can see which collaborator made each change in a group document. Of course, the slightly less elegant Undo and Redo functions are always available as well!

Revision history
Today, 4:32 PM
Anne C
March 1, 4:08 PM
Anne C
February 28, 10:25 PM
Anne C
February 28, 7:51 PM
Anne C
February 24, 10:21 PM
Anne C
February 23, 10:53 PM
Anne C
February 23, 8:18 PM
Anne C
February 22, 6:15 PM
Anne C
February 21, 8:38 PM
Anne C
Show changes
Show more detailed revisions

Dealing with Other File Formats

Fortunately, you can edit Microsoft Office files in Google apps like Google Docs. Just open the file and edit away. Google Docs can also open files with .ODT, .DOT, .HTML, and .TXT file extensions, though there's always a chance that the original formatting may not survive the conversion entirely intact.

Add-ons

Most of the Google productivity apps include the ability to add on functionality, typically designed by third party developers. You can search for add-ons by clicking the Add-ons menu item at the top of the screen. Click Get add-ons to start searching for the additional functions you need. For example, in Docs, you can install add-ons that reveal the document's structure in a table of contents presentation in the sidebar. There's even a Sudoku add-on for Sheets!

GOOGLE SHEETS

Google Sheets is Google's answer to Microsoft Excel. If you're familiar with any spreadsheet program, you should feel pretty at home in Sheets. Like almost every other spreadsheet program, Google Sheets will do all the heavy lifting for you when it comes to calculations. Entering formulas in

Google Sheets is reasonably similar to Excel. Just type = at the beginning of a cell and then fill in your formula. Of course, there are some minor syntactical differences you'll need to get the hang of, but it's nothing too difficult. Sheets will help you build your formulas by giving you input examples, and you can create charts from your data and define custom sorting and filtering rules.

GOOGLE SLIDES

Google Slides is a presentation app, like Microsoft PowerPoint. Slides includes several prepackaged presentation themes to get you started, or you can begin with a blank slate. Your completed presentation can be downloaded as a PowerPoint, PDF, image, scalable vector graphic or plain text file, making Slides presentations compatible with just about any environment. There's also a very useful "Publish to the web" feature available in the File menu that will generate a public URL that you can share with your colleagues and/or the entire world. You can also embed Slides presentations in web pages or blog posts. To do this, go to File and Publish to the Web.

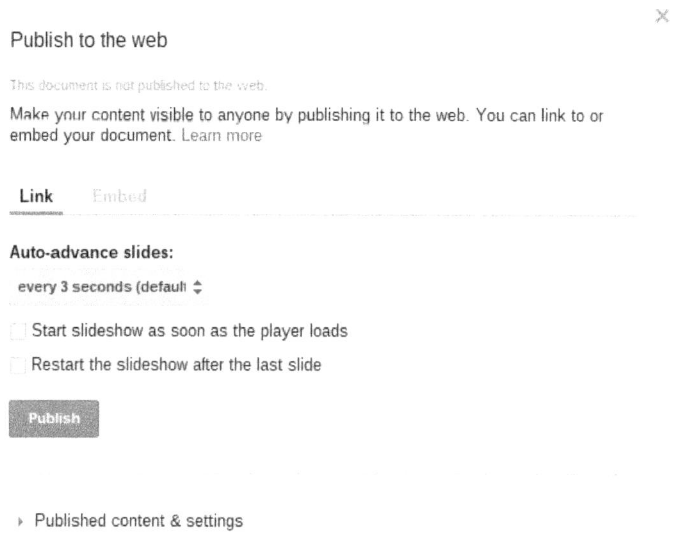

SCRATCHPAD

Scratchpad is meant for small, simple document creation (like Notes on Mac or Notepad on Windows). Things like grocery and to-do lists that don't necessarily need advanced formatting or structure for later publishing work well with Scratchpad.

GOOGLE+ AND HANGOUTS

Google+ began life as Google's attempt at a social network. It was their answer to Facebook and Twitter. If you are reading this wondering what Google+ is then you probably can tell they didn't quite accomplish everything they hoped. It will, in fact, be discontinued shortly.

Google+ has been out for over six years, which may surprise you. It certainly isn't Google's most widely used product, but it has grown in popularity since it came out and has evolved a lot. Sharing photos, videos, and more are made possible through the network. For businesses, the most important feature is Hangouts—a Skype-like service that lets you have group video calls and share screens.

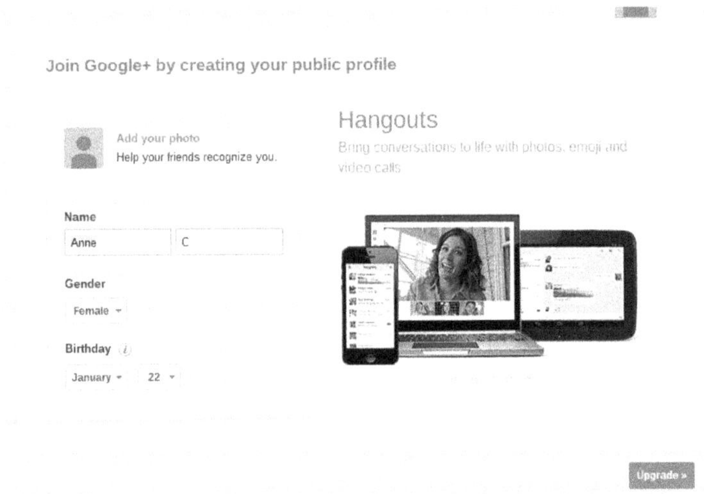

To sign up for Google+, you'll first need to enter your name, gender, and birthday. Next, Google+ will suggest people you may know, based on any existing Gmail contacts you've entered. Use the Add button to add them to your circles (in Google+ you'll organize your contacts into circles, like friends, college buddies, frenemies, etc.).

Next, Google+ will suggest some topics for you to follow that you might be interested in. Finally, you'll be able to update your profile by adding a photo and some additional personal details. Then you'll be all set to start using Google+!

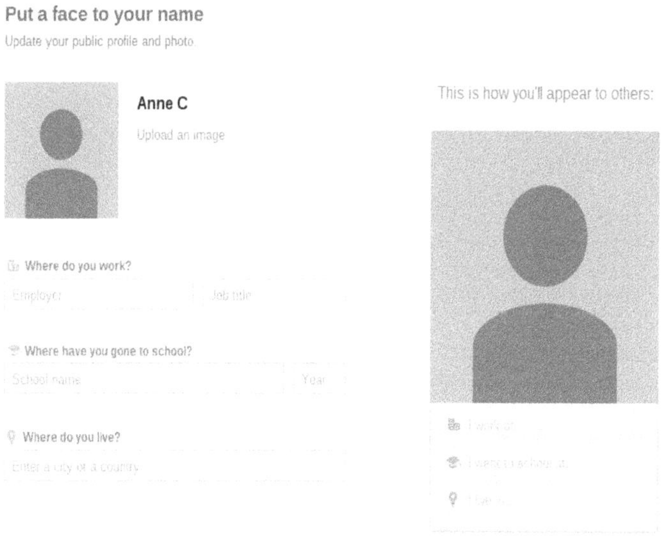

Inside the Google+ app, there are a few things to be aware of. In the top left corner, you'll see a button labeled Home. Click this button to expand the Google+ menu.

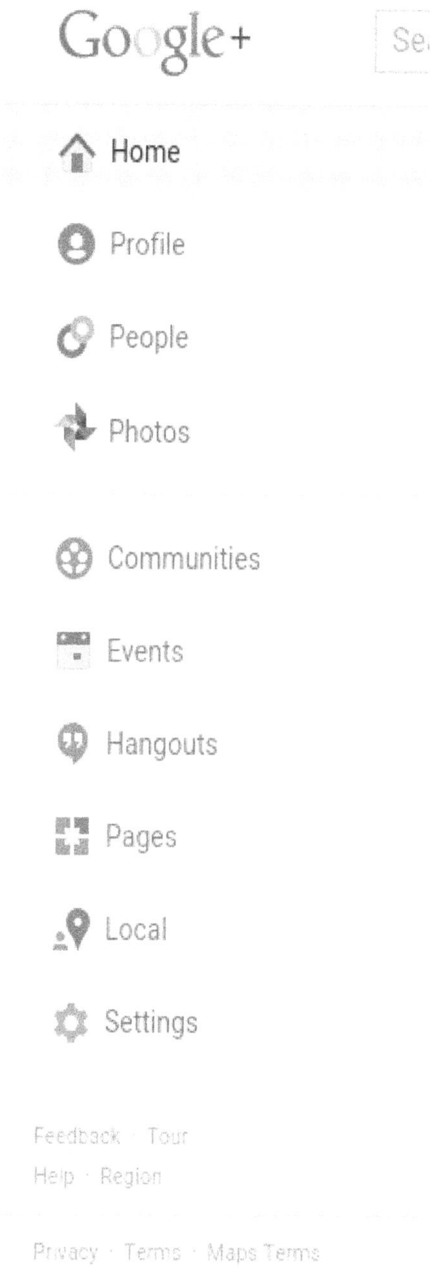
Google+
Home
Profile
People
Photos
Communities
Events
Hangouts
Pages
Local
Settings
Feedback · Tour
Help · Region
Privacy · Terms · Maps Terms

This menu should be familiar to Facebook users. You'll see options to get to your profile and edit it if necessary, as well as links to the people you follow and the photos you've posted. You'll also find Communities, Events, Hangouts, Pages, Local info, and Settings.

Posting in Google+

You can post various items in Google+, just like Facebook. You can add text, photos, links, videos, events (which you can invite your contacts to, of course), and polls.

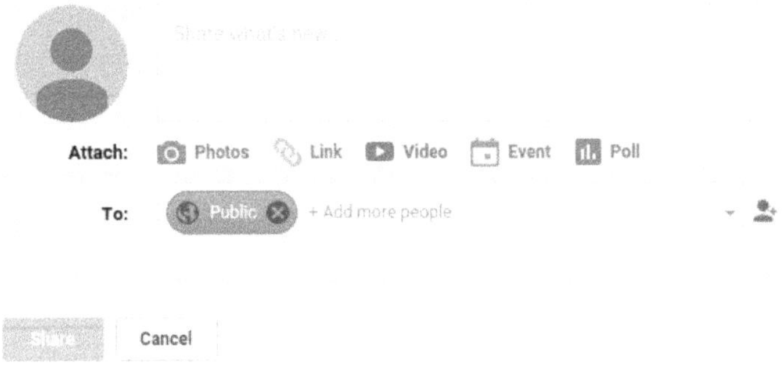

Google+ posts can be shared publicly, with certain people, or Google+ circles using the To: field in the post dialog box.

Hangouts

Without a doubt, Hangouts is the most successful aspect of Google+. It's like everything that was great about a late 1990s chat room combined with the power of Skype-like services. A Hangout generates a URL. Participants can use that link to leave and come back to a Hangout at any time, just like a chat room.

You can start a Hangout from inside Google+ or Gmail, or you can use the dedicated Hangouts app. To start a Hangout, you'll enter friends' names (if they're contacts in Google+) or email addresses (if they're not). You can also add entire Google+ circles or make a Hangout open to the entire public. If you'd rather have a private call, though, just add a single name.

Hangouts takes advantage of your Chromebook's built-in microphone and camera, just like Skype or FaceTime. It's easy to use and, as long as you have a free Wi-Fi connection, completely free.

GMAIL

Gmail is Google's proprietary email client, and I think it's the best of the bunch when it comes to web email hosts. If you've set up a new Google account for your Chromebook, then your Gmail address is your username plus @gmail.com. If you need to check your Gmail account from another computer, visit gmail.com and enter your Google account username and password to sign in. You can open Gmail in any browser, like Internet Explorer or Firefox.

Opening the Gmail app on your Chromebook will take you straight to your Gmail inbox.

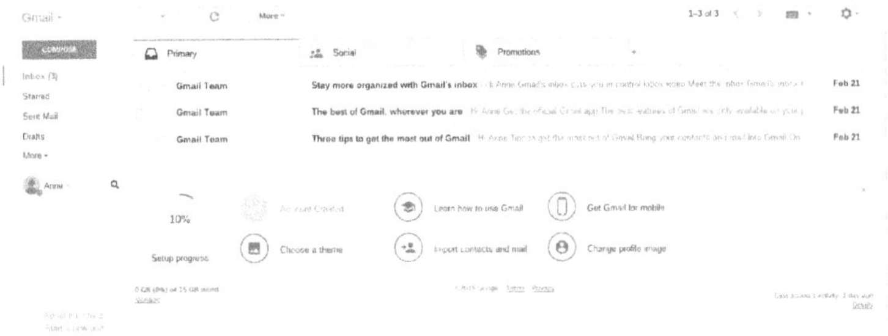

Gmail presorts your mail into three tabs—Primary, Social, and Promotions. This is a great way to tame an unruly inbox. All your Facebook notifications show up under Social, and those daily emails from that store you went to once will appear under Promotions, helping you focus on the email you most likely really want to read.

Of course, occasional mistakes will happen. If a message appears under the wrong tab, just drag it to the tab that you'd like future messages from that sender to appear under.

You'll notice the first time you open Gmail that the Chromebook Gmail app guides you through some basic setup tasks that will help you really get to know Gmail, if you don't already. You can choose a theme, import contacts, work through a tutorial, install Gmail on a mobile phone, and add a new profile image. Take some time and work through these steps—you'll be glad you did, and it makes for a great introduction to Gmail.

Sending Email in Gmail

To start a new email message, open Gmail and click the red Compose button in the left menu.

This brings up the Compose pop-up screen, which allows you to compose your email while keeping an eye on your inbox. Enter the email address of your recipient in the To field and the subject of your email in the Subject field. If you need to add a CC (Carbon Copy, which is visible to other recipients) or BCC (Blind Carbon Copy—invisible to other recipients) recipient, click the gray Cc Bcc text in the top right corner of the New Message window. Then, of course, your message goes in the big blank area. When you're finished writing, click the blue Send button in the lower left corner of the New Message window to send your email.

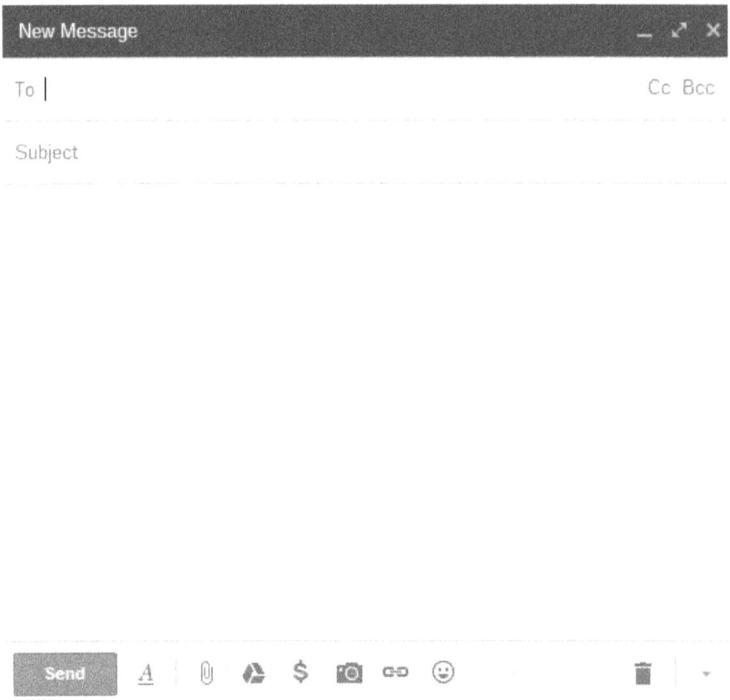

Gmail also makes it easy to format your email and add attachments and multimedia. Next to the Send button, the A icon will display options for formatting text (bold, italics, font choice, etc.). Next, the paper clip icon opens up a dialog box that lets you browse your Chromebook for files to attach to your message, like PDFs, Google Docs documents, etc. If you have a file in Drive that you'd like to insert, use the Drive icon instead of the paper clip. You can use the $ icon as a sort of Google version of PayPal, if you have a credit card or bank account set up in your Google account. The camera icon lets you add images to your email—either as attachments or inside the email itself. Next, the chain link icon lets you add links to your email. If you type a full website address, like www.google.com, Gmail will recognize the link and will send it as such. Finally, you can insert Google emoticons using the smiley face icon.

Gmail saves draft messages for you automatically. If you accidentally close a message you're working on, you'll find it safe and sound in your Drafts folder on the left. However, if you decide you don't want to save a draft message, use the trashcan icon in the lower right corner of the New Message window to delete it.

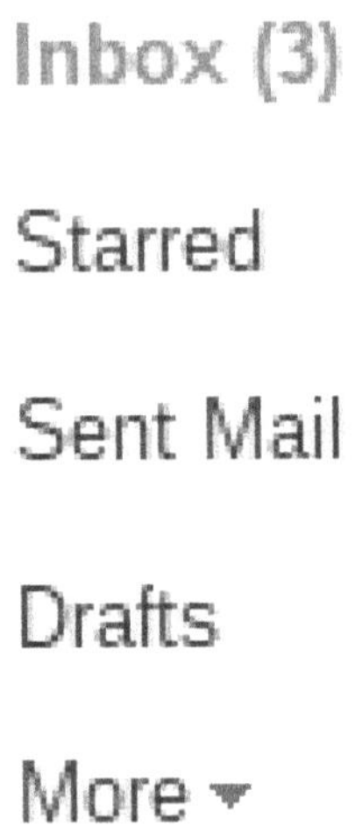

The downward arrow in the far lower right corner of the New Message window gives you a few more options for managing your message. Perhaps the most immediately useful thing here is the spell-check function, but it's good to know how to print a draft or send it to full screen as well. We'll talk about labels in just a minute.

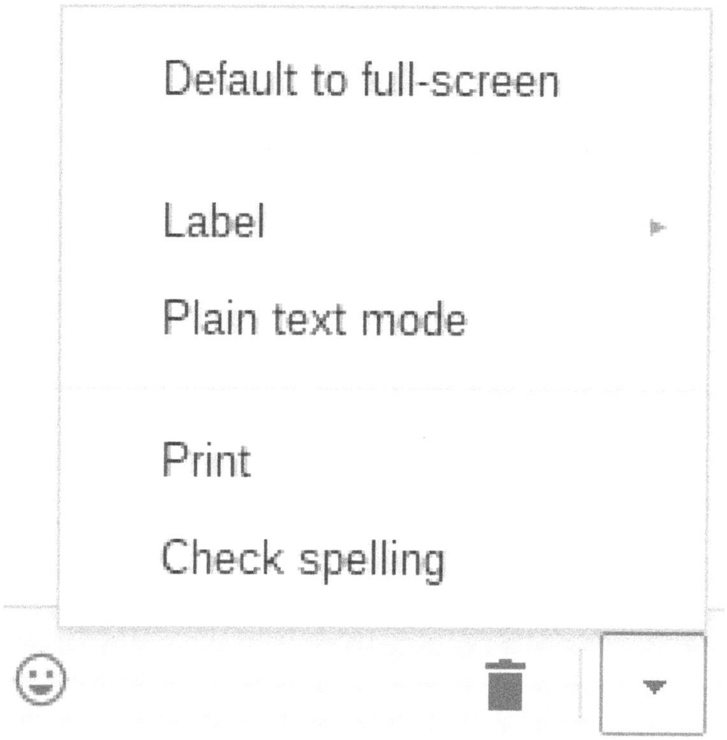

Managing Email

Gmail makes it exceptionally easy to deal with the daily barrage of incoming messages in this day and age. The toolbar pictured below appears at the top of every email, and will appear when emails are selected in the inbox or a folder.

When you're finished with a message, you can delete it, either from inside the opened message or by clicking the checkbox next to the email in your inbox, and then clicking the trashcan icon. However, Gmail makes it easy to get messages out of your inbox, thus decreasing clutter without actually deleting them, thanks to its Archive feature. The archive button is the first icon in the Gmail toolbar. When you archive a message, it disappears from your inbox, but not from your account. You can search for it at any time using Gmail's search bar at the top of the Gmail screen.

Of course, sometimes archiving isn't quite nuanced enough, and that's where favorites and labels come in. To make an email a favorite, just click the star icon next to it. You can then get to all of your starred emails by clicking Starred in the left menu.

Labels are an easy way to categorize your email. You can add as many custom labels as you like in the left menu. Just click More in the left menu, and then click Create New Label at the bottom.

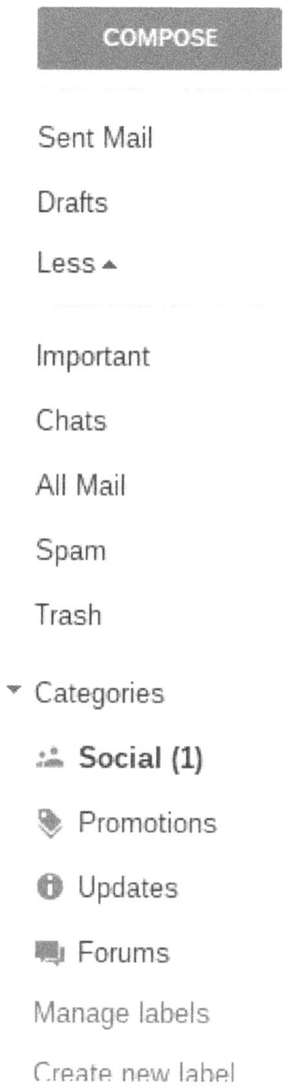

To apply a label (or labels) to a message, click the Label icon in the top toolbar. A dropdown menu will appear that gives you a list of all of your existing labels. Click on one to apply it, or type in a new label in the box to set it up and add it to the message.

Contacts

You may have noticed that there's no dedicated contact app in Chromebook. That's because, between Gmail and Google+, there's no real need for one. Gmail is an excellent contacts manager in its own right, and Google+ adds additional contacts capabilities.

To manage contacts in Gmail, click the red Gmail text in the top left corner. A dropdown menu will appear, allowing you to switch to Contacts or Tasks view. All of your Google+ contacts will be automatically added, but you can add non-Google+ information and people as well. To manually add a new contact, click the red New Contact button.

You can then add names, pictures, emails, phone numbers, addresses—basically, as much or as little information as you want. To add a field other than the ones displayed, just click the Add button underneath all of the text entry fields. There's plenty to choose from!

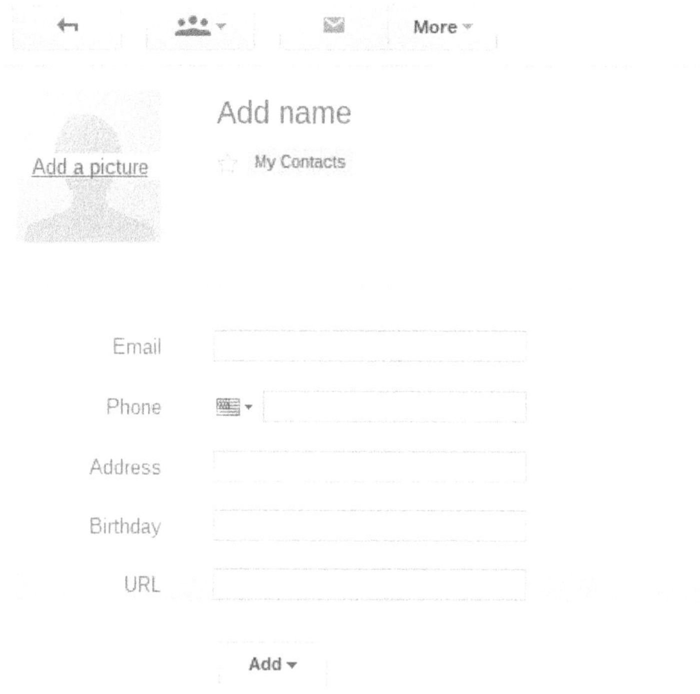

Chat/Calls

You can start chats and initiate calls from within Gmail itself. At the very bottom of the left menu, you'll see three icons—Hangouts, Chats, and Phone Calls. Click each one to view any contacts you may have that have these features enabled.

You can start a Hangout, text-based chat, or phone call by clicking a contact's name.

Tasks

Much like Microsoft Outlook, Gmail includes a Task list. You can add items to your task list, add new lists altogether, and set due dates. It's a very simple task manager, but like everything else in Gmail, it's accessible from any machine with an Internet browser.

YOUTUBE

We can't imagine the modern Internet without YouTube. YouTube is very tightly integrated with your Google account, so you're automatically signed in whenever you open the YouTube app.

Watching Videos

Perhaps the most obvious thing you'll want to do with the YouTube app is watch streaming videos online. This is easy and extremely addictive! You can search for videos using the YouTube search bar at the top of the YouTube app page, or you can browse around the featured videos underneath.

When you've found a video you'd like to watch, simply click it in the search results list. It'll start to play. Note that many popular YouTube videos, and/or videos that use copyrighted material like songs, may play an ad before the video starts. Try not to be too annoyed—this is how YouTube remains free and full of hilarious parodies, remixes, and reinterpretations that make it so much fun!

There are media controls in the lower left corner of the YouTube player window where you can pause the video, control the volume, and see the elapsed and remaining time. In the lower right corner, you'll find some additional features, including (from left to right) Watch Later, Settings (where you can adjust the speed and quality of the video playback depending on your system and connection speed), Theatre Mode and Full Screen. Theatre Mode is sort of halfway between the normal YouTube display and Full Screen—try it out to see if it's for you. Full Screen, of course, is the best way to get your computer to mimic a television.

To the right of the video player, you'll see a list of related videos. This is great if you're entertaining yourself with one of the millions of YouTube memes out there (literal music videos, inappropriate music for movies, and Sharky the Pit Bull are some of my classic favorites).

You can thumbs up or thumbs down a video, or comment on it to take advantage of YouTube's social features. Scroll down to see the comments underneath the player. I'm not going to lie to you here. YouTube comments can be...rough. I ask in the name of a brighter Internet future that if you're going to participate in YouTube commentary that you 1) don't feed the trolls, and 2) don't be a troll! Trolls, for the record, are Internet users who say inflammatory and frequently extremely offensive things for the purpose of eliciting a reaction, and you're probably going to come across them if you spend much time on the site.

Account Features

There's more to YouTube than simply browsing around and watching online videos. Using your Google account, you can create playlists of YouTube videos, subscribe to other users' channels, access a list of your recently viewed videos, and create a Watch Later list for when you just don't have time for that twenty minute documentary on urban beekeeping but are really interested. You'll find all of these options in the YouTube menu to the left of the main content area. You can click the menu button next to the YouTube logo in the top left corner to hide and reveal these extra features as needed.

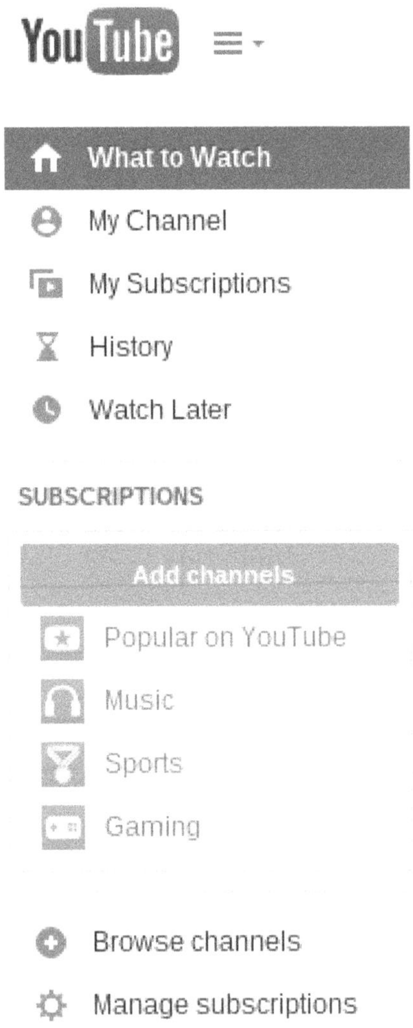
What to Watch
My Channel
My Subscriptions
History
Watch Later
SUBSCRIPTIONS
Add channels
Popular on YouTube
Music
Sports
Gaming
Browse channels
Manage subscriptions

To subscribe to a YouTube channel, locate the channel's owner on a video page, or, if you know the owner's name, just search for it using the YouTube search bar. Then, on their profile page, click the red Subscribe button. You'll then find new content from that user under Subscriptions in the YouTube menu.

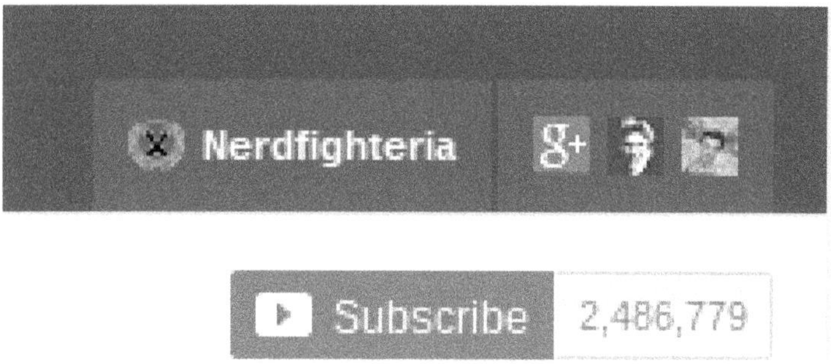

To create a playlist of YouTube videos, click Add to underneath the creators' names on the video's page. Before you can take advantage of this, though, you'll need to set up your Google+ profile and your YouTube channel page. The first time you click Add to you'll be prompted to set all of this up if you haven't already.

Uploading Videos

If you'd like to upload your own videos to YouTube, just click the Upload button in the top right corner.

You'll need to set up your Google+ profile and your YouTube channel page before you can upload, but after that you can easily upload and share your videos. Videos can be private or only shared with certain people. You can also choose to enable or disable public comments, depending on your preference.

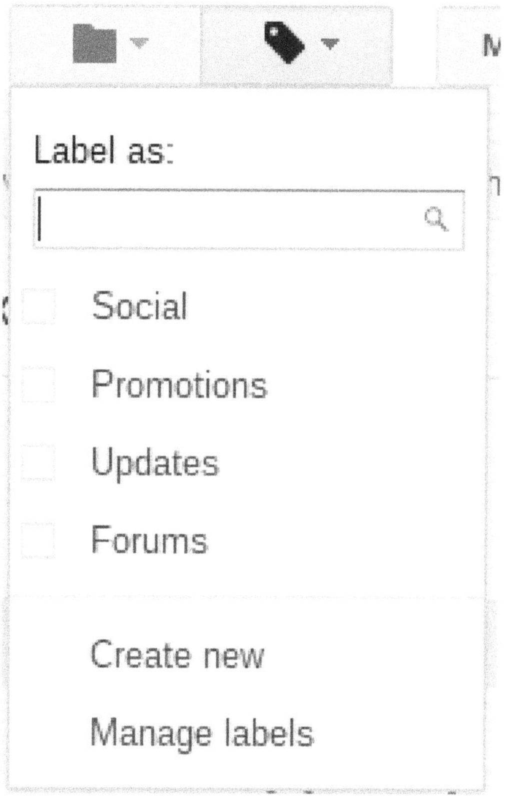

You can click on your labels in the left menu to see all messages categorized with them. You can also search for labels in the Gmail search bar.

CALCULATOR

The Calculator app is a simple utility and a rare example of an app that doesn't open inside a Chrome window. It performs basic calculations—no more, no less. It's nice to have a calculator that appears outside of all your other Chrome tabs and windows, though, and you may want to consider pinning it to your Chromebook's shelf if you find yourself using it time and time again.

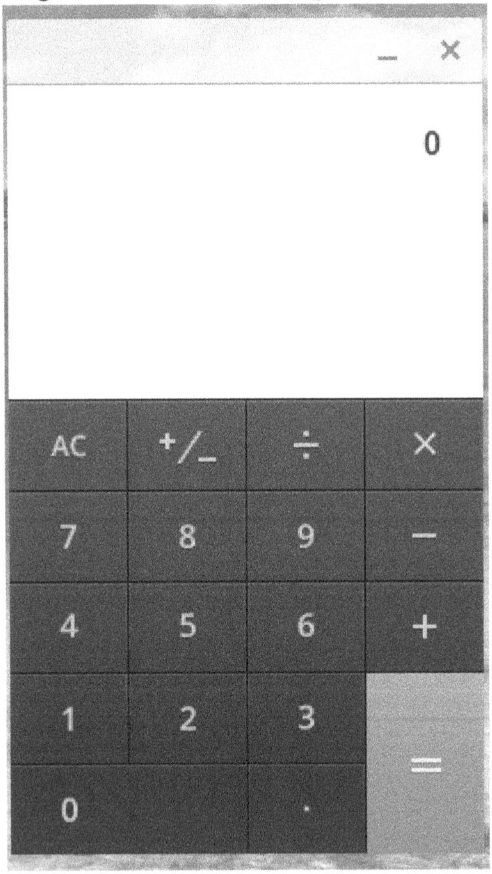

CAMERA

The Pixel is not the device you want to use to take stunning professional photos. It's worth noting, however, that there is a Camera app on the computer that can take very basic photos and videos.

To open it, go to the Launcher and then type "Camera."

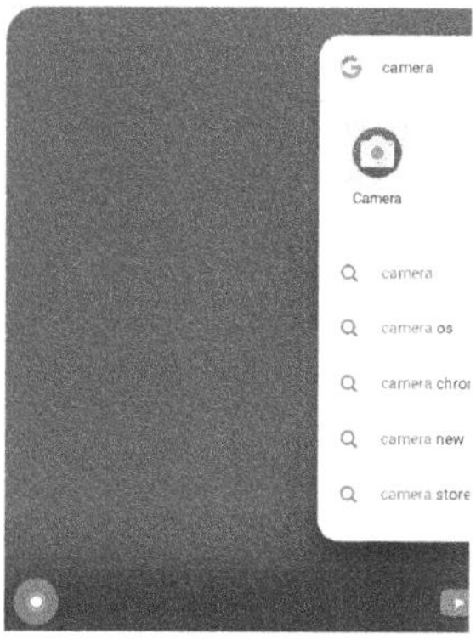

The app is very stripped down. On the right side are the three different modes: Video, Photo and Square.

On the left are the three basic tools you can use with the app: mirror (which flips the camera), grid, and timer.

In the upper right corner, there's also a config icon.

When you tap the config icon, you'll have a few additional settings.

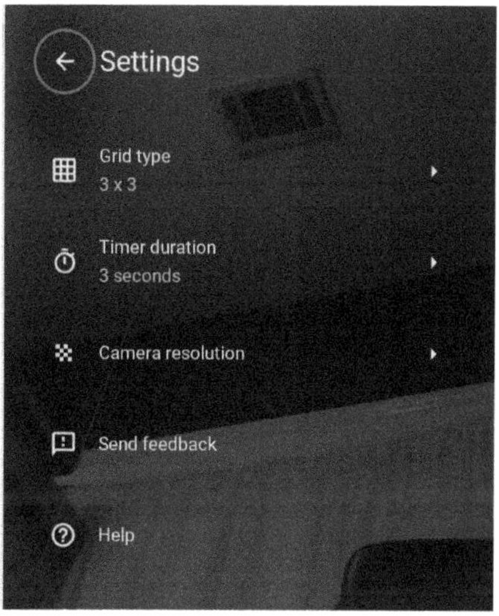

CHROME REMOTE DESKTOP

Chrome Remote Desktop (CRD) is similar in function to Windows Remote Desktop and Apple Remote Desktop. Basically, it allows you to view and control a different computer or device remotely. It's incredibly helpful for Instructional Technology (IT) professionals and for getting help with your system.

For Chrome Remote Desktop to work, both machines must be running the CRD app, which can be installed in Chrome in any operating system, as long as the Google Chrome browser is installed. To open a connection, the remote user needs to open the CRD app and click Share. This will generate an access code which the remote user will give to you. Enter the access code into CRD on your Chromebook, and you'll be able to see and control the remote machine.

GOOGLE+ PHOTOS

The Google+ Photos app is your Chromebook's photo manager. It's not entirely unlike Apple's iPhoto, but it is very tightly integrated with Google+, for better or worse. Google+ Photos helps you consolidate your photos, organize them and share them through Google+.

To get started, open the app using the Apps button. You'll need to sign up for Google+ if you haven't already done so. From there, you can import photos from your Google+ account, your Chromebook, or Google Drive by clicking the Add Photos button in the top right corner. You can then organize your photos into albums, share them through Google+, delete them, or save them to your Chromebook or your Google Drive account.

The Photos app includes the ability to rotate the photo and/or enhance it using the Enhance tool, which appears when you move your mouse over the photo. This is an automatic fix rather than a set of manual features. For serious photo editing, I recommend Pixlr Editor or another photo app from the Web Store.

GOOGLE KEEP

Google Keep is a note-taking app that aims to compete with products like Microsoft OneNote or Evernote. You can add notes and reminders lists that will sync with the online version of Keep at keep.google.com. There's also an Android app that you can download for your smartphone or tablet.

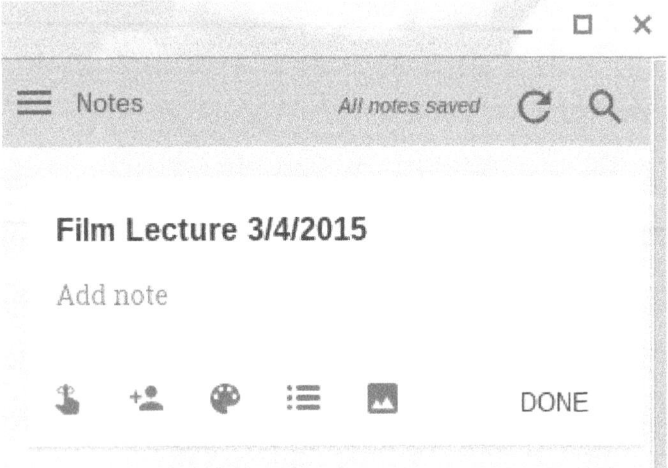

Notes in Keep can include lists and images, and you can share them with others. It's a handy way to keep yourself organized, and it's a quick note-taking app for those times when you don't need all the bells and whistles of Google Docs.

GOOGLE MAPS AND GOOGLE MY MAPS

Google Maps is, in my opinion, the best free online maps service in the game, and it's built right into your Chromebook.

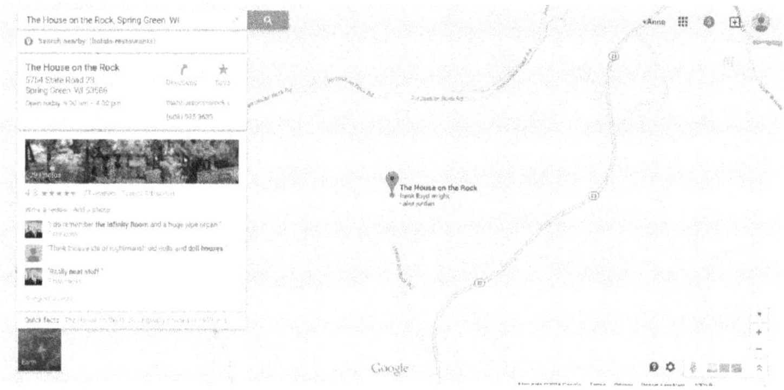

To use Google Maps, type the address, town or place name (The House on the Rock, Yellowstone National Park, etc.), into the search box in the top left corner. From there, you can get directions to that address by clicking Directions, or you can save the location for later reference. In the example above, you can see that Google Maps also pulled reviews and contact information for me, since I searched for a popular tourist destination.

In the bottom left corner, you will see a box labeled Earth. Clicking this box will toggle Google Earth—a beautiful satellite mode that will give you a photographic aerial view of your mapped area. You can switch back to Map mode by clicking the Map square in the bottom left corner.

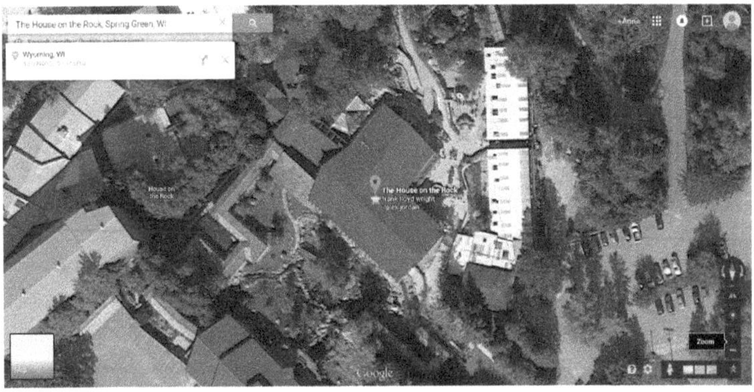

In the bottom right corner of the screen, you'll find a few controls for adjusting your Google Maps experience. The Target button is a shortcut to your current location. Click it to get a map of your immediate surroundings. Beneath it, the + and - buttons let you zoom in and out. You can zoom out to a planetary view if you like!

The little yellow man in the controls area is the Google Streetview operator. Drag him from this menu to a spot on the map to enter Streetview. Streetview is a great way to check out a neighborhood or to explore the world a little. The screenshot below is the view from beneath the Eiffel Tower.

Google My Maps

The Google My Maps app is somewhat confusingly named, but it's extremely useful if you ever need to share directions with a large group of people. It's basically Google Maps, but slightly remixed in such a way that users can save maps in Google Drive and import layers of data into the Maps interface. For example, you might have a spreadsheet listing addresses that you'd like to add. You can also add placemarks and give them your own description, or draw lines, or add Google Maps routes and directions. Once your custom map is complete, you can share it using a generated link that can be copied and pasted wherever you need it, or through email, Google+, Facebook, and Twitter. This is a very handy feature for invitations or websites.

GOOGLE FORMS

Google Forms is a form generator that works closely with Google Sheets. If you've ever used Survey Monkey before, you should feel right at home in Forms. Your Forms questions can include multiple choice, text, checkboxes, scales, grids, dates and times, and you can make as many answers required as you like. Once your form is complete, you can invite people to fill it out through a URL or through email invitations. Responses will be automatically recorded in a Google Sheets spreadsheet for analysis (though you can turn this off if you'd prefer to keep all responses inside the Forms app for some reason).

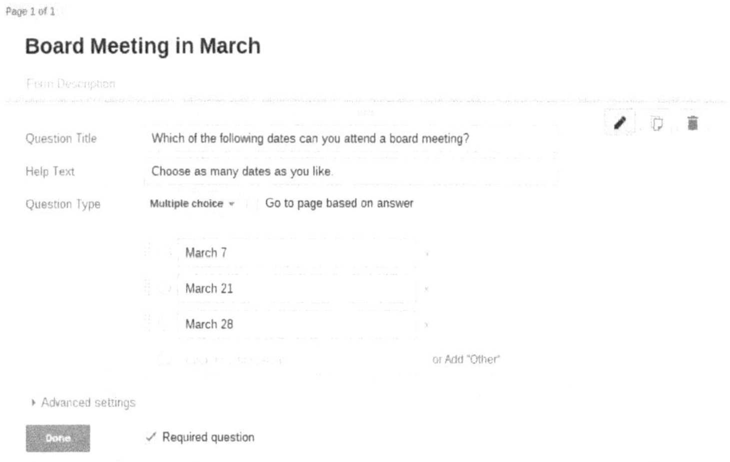

GOOGLE DRAWINGS

The Google Drawings app allows you to create and annotate images. You can also insert text boxes, shapes, and lines. The freeform drawing tool is called Scribbles, and you'll find it under Insert > Line. Drawings shouldn't be compared to giants like Photoshop or Illustrator. Its closest relative is probably Microsoft Paint. Of course, any images you create in Drawings are saved in Drive, meaning it's very easy to insert them into other Drive apps, like Google Slides or Google Docs.

PLAY MUSIC, PLAY BOOKS, AND PLAY MOVIES

These three media apps make it possible to enjoy music, books, and movies purchased from the Google Play Store and from elsewhere on your Chromebook.

Play Music

The Play Music app includes an optional subscription that gives you access to millions of streaming songs without any ads. First time users generally get some sort of free trial offer, but after that it costs $9.99 a month.

If you decide to use the Standard version of Play Music, you'll then be given the option to upload your music from other sources, including iTunes. To do this, you may need to navigate to

Google Play Music from the device that has your tunes on it, which is probably not your relatively low-memory Chromebook. However, once you've uploaded your library (from anywhere), you can enjoy it streaming through Play Music on your Chromebook and on most other devices by installing the Play Music app. You can upload up to 50,000 songs free of charge.

Play Books

Play Books is an ebook app that's half bookshelf and half bookstore. At the top of the Play Books app, you'll see two links—My Books and Shop Books. Any books you've purchased through the Shop link (or through the Google Play Store on a different computer) will appear under My Books. Buying books is identical to buying apps or extensions. If you don't already have a credit card number on file with Google, you'll be prompted to enter one. Of course, there are a number of classics and other free titles in the Play Store, so there's no need to whip out the plastic if you don't want to!

Any books you buy through Play Books will be available on your Android smartphone or tablet as well, and the Play Books app will keep everything synced up. This means that no matter what device you're using to read, your current read will open to exactly where you left off.

Play Movies

The Play Movies app allows you to enjoy movies and television shows purchased through the Google Play Store. Just like the Play Books app, Play Movies includes a Shop link where you can find streaming video to watch.

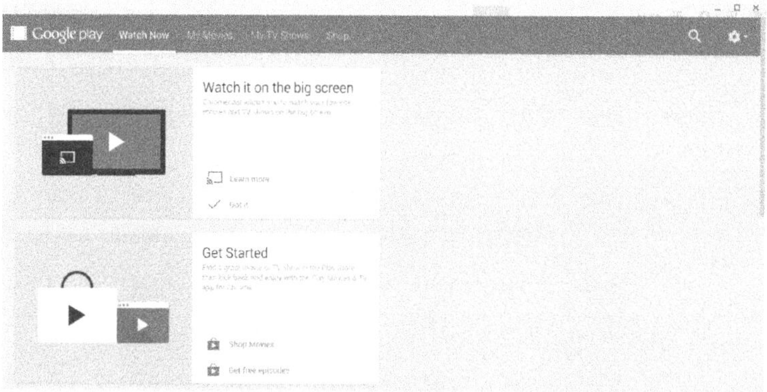

Google Play movies and television shows can be bought (you can stream them as many times as you like) or rented (you can only stream them during a certain amount of time). There are often pretty good deals on the Play Store—for example, at the time of writing, Star Trek was on offer in HD for just $4.99.

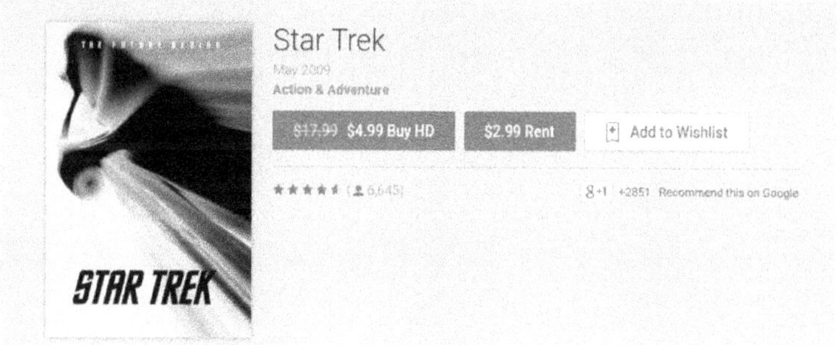

GOOGLE CALENDAR

Google Calendar is a great calendar tool, particularly since it's so widely used and importable into a variety of other calendaring systems. It's easy to use, available through google.com/calendar on any computer with a web browser, and will notify you of upcoming events so you never miss a thing.

Adding a New Calendar Event

To add a new event to Google Calendar, click the red Create button in the top left corner.

Enter as much or as little information about your event as you need. Keep in mind that Google Calendar has some powerful time management features to help keep you on track. It will send notifications before your event, at an interval of your choosing. You can also set recurring events by clicking the "Repeat" checkbox.

Adding and Sharing Calendars

The Google Calendar system includes the ability to set up multiple calendars. Maybe you'd like to have one personal calendar and then a shared family calendar or a team project calendar. To add a new calendar, click the boxed downward-pointing arrow to the right of the My Calendars heading in the left menu. This will take you to the New Calendar setup screen. At the bottom, you'll see options for controlling your calendar's privacy and inviting people to view and/or add to the calendar.

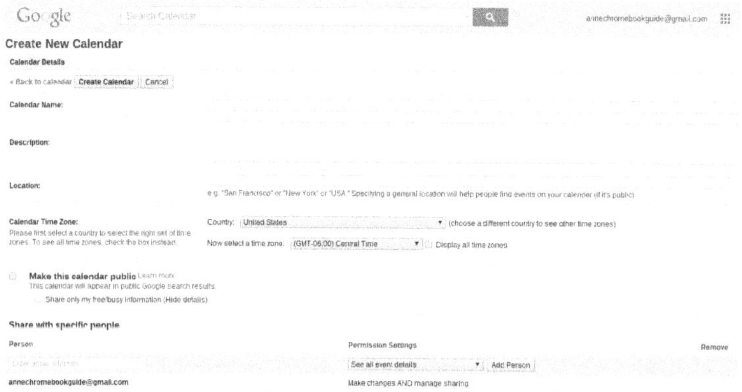

Hiding Calendars

I've found that it's very easy to get enthusiastic about calendars, only to find yourself drowning in calendar entries. Fortunately, it's easy to temporarily hide calendars to help clean up your view. To hide a calendar, just click the little colored square next to its name in the My Calendars list. This won't delete anything, but it will hide all events associated with that calendar so you can focus on the events that need your attention.

[6]

MAKING IT YOUR OWN WITH CUSTOMIZATIONS

This chapter will cover:

- Changing the Appearance
- Device
- Searching
- People
- Date and Time
- Privacy
- Web Content
- Languages
- Downloads

- HTTPS/SSL Certificates
- Google Cloud Print
- Startup
- Accessibility
- Powerwash and Reset
- Supervised Accounts
- Troubleshooting

In this section, we'll talk about several ways you can customize your Chromebook to suit your unique needs and personality. There are quite a few useful tweaks available for Chromebook, and I'll walk you through them all here. I'll also show you how to manage user accounts on your Chromebook, including children's accounts, and give you a few tips for troubleshooting and finding help.

To open your Chromebook settings, click the area of the screen that displays the time, wireless connection, battery, and your profile picture in the bottom right corner. Then click Settings. We're going to examine each heading that appears on this screen.

CHANGING THE APPEARANCE

The Appearance heading in Settings covers, well, the appearance of your Chromebook. Here you can set your desktop wallpaper to a custom image by clicking Set Wallpaper. This will open up a dialog box where you can browse your Chromebook for the image file you'd like to use. You can also click the Get Themes button to be taken to the Themes area of the Chrome Web Store. Themes add a graphic layer to your Chrome window—an image or color for new tab windows and colors and designs for the menu area. There are plenty of fun themes to choose from, and if you change your mind about any of them, you can always click Reset to Default Theme to go back to Chrome's original appearance.

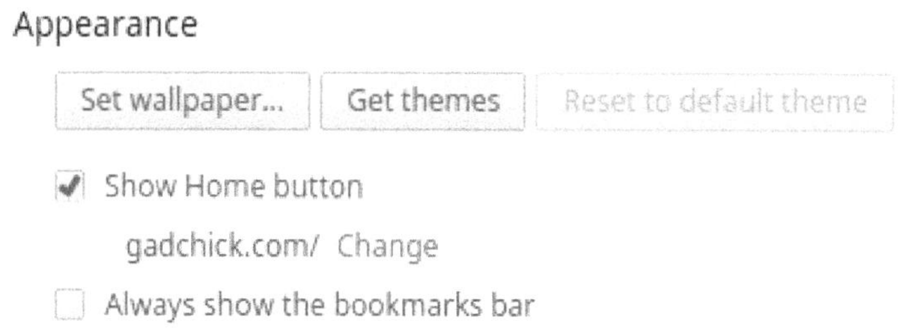

You can also set a home page here if you like. First, click Show Home button to tell Chrome to show the Home button in your Chrome browser as a special shortcut to your home page. Click Change to add a new home page. This is the page that will be displayed every time you open Chrome.

Finally, you can choose to always show the bookmarks bar in Chrome here as well.

DEVICE

The Device heading is a pretty important Settings area, even if it's a little bit of a catchall. There are some really useful options and features tucked away here.

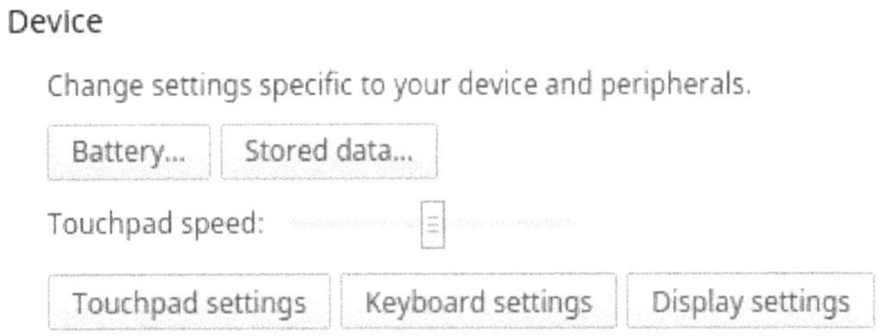

First, you can take a look at what's using your battery by clicking the Battery button. This is a great way to maximize your Chromebook's battery even further if you need to. Just close the apps that are sucking up the most juice.

The Stored Data button is also a fascinating glimpse into what Chrome is doing with every page and app you visit or use. Check out what my Chromebook has to say about weather.com.

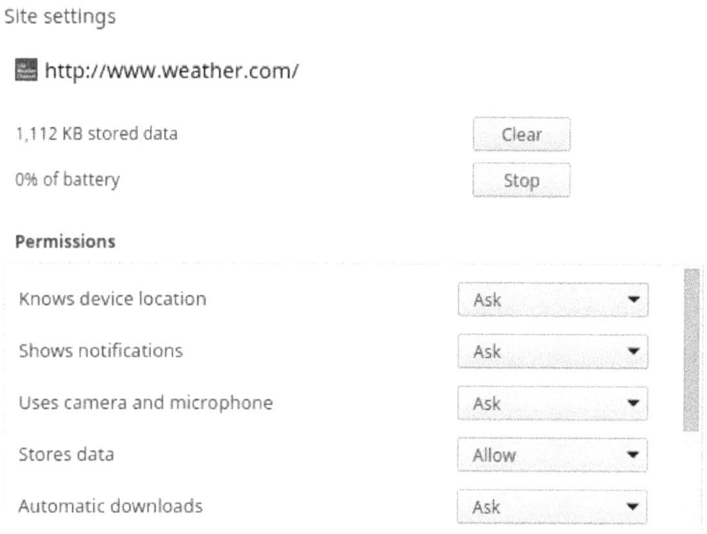

I can see how much stored data from this site is eating into my hard disc (in this case, not very much), as well as how much of the battery it's using. Right now, it's not running, so it requires 0% of my battery. Then I can see a fairly extensive list of permissions for the site, and change them as I see fit. For this example, I may want to allow this site to know our Chromebook's location so that it will always give me the weather of our current spot.

Underneath the battery and stored data information, you'll find some options for configuring your touchpad, keyboard, and display. You can adjust your touchpad's speed to match that of your fingers using the slider, and you can also change the direction the page moves when you scroll and enable or disable tap-to-click. By clicking Keyboard, you can view the shortcut display mentioned earlier in the book, and you can also change the behavior of certain keyboard keys if you like—namely Search, CTRL, and ALT.

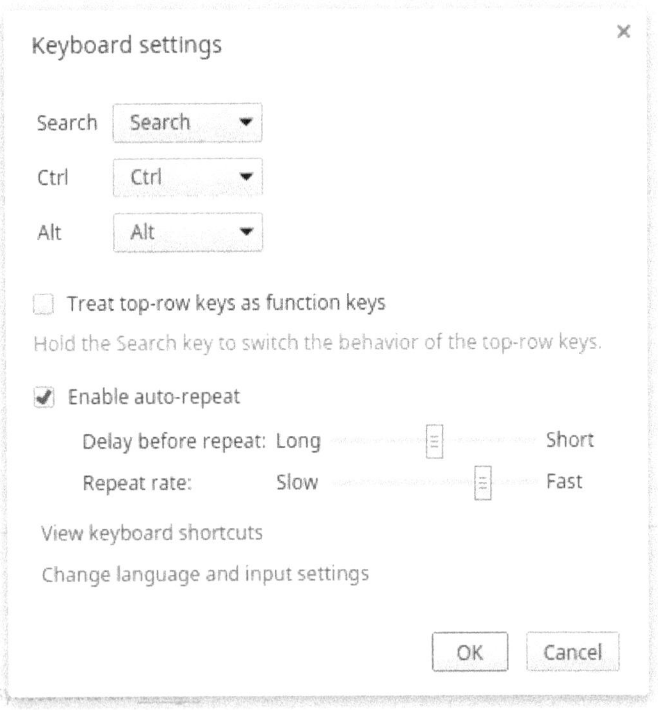

SEARCHING

One of my favorite things about Google products is their flexibility. It would stand to reason that the proprietary Google OS based on Google's browser would limit users to the Google search engine for the Chrome omnibox, but that's not the case. In the Search heading, you can change Chrome's search engine to Yahoo!, Bing, Ask, or AOL.

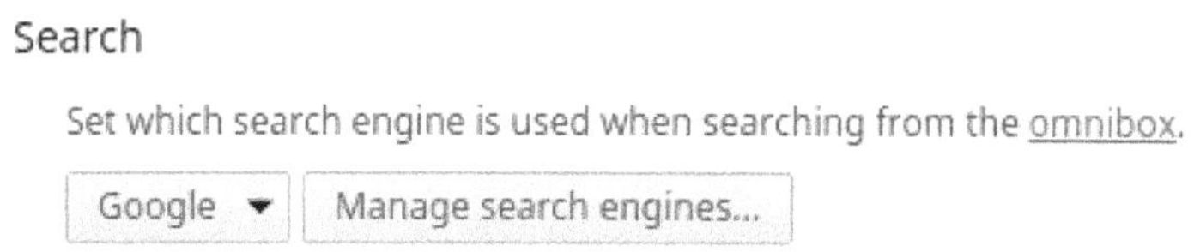

The Manage Search Engines button finds additional search engines, like YouTube search, for example. You can add these highly specific searches as your omnibox default if you'd like (though for most users we do recommend sticking with a general internet-wide search engine).

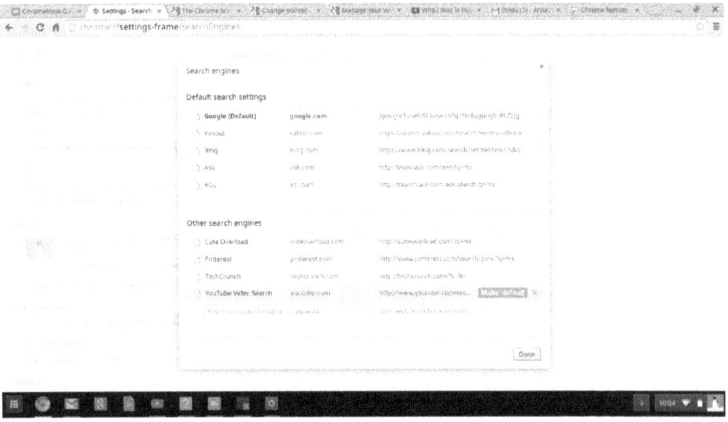

PEOPLE

Under the People heading, you can accomplish two important tasks. First, you can manage what aspects of your Chromebook sync with your Google account by clicking Advanced Sync Settings. By default, everything is selected, but you can adjust as needed. You can also choose how you'd like Google Chrome to encrypt your data.

The other feature under People is the ability to manage logins on your Chromebook. More than one Google user can sign in, and you can manage other users as needed. You can decide whether or not to enable a Guest account and supervised users (which we'll talk about in more detail shortly) and whether or not to restrict sign in to certain users. You can also add users to your Chromebook here.

At this point, you'll need to click Show Advanced Settings to see the rest of the Chrome settings menu!

DATE AND TIME

There's not much here besides the ability to change your time zone and switch your system clock to 24-hour time. Chrome will set the date and time automatically based on your time zone.

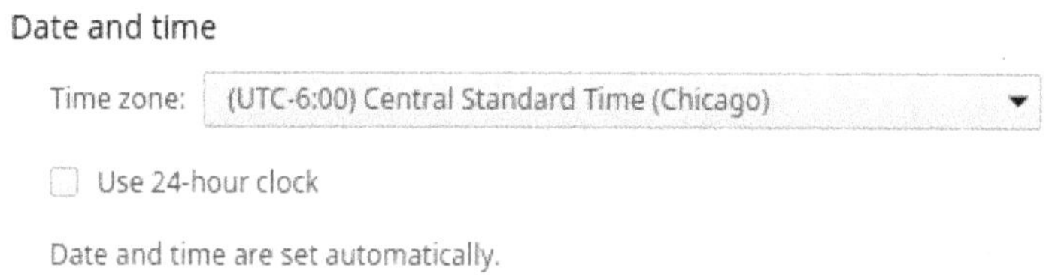

PRIVACY

Your privacy settings give you some control over how much information your Chromebook shares with the rest of the world. Google uses quite a few prediction services in order to load pages fast and get you where you want to go, but you may not want all of them accessing your personal information, search engine terms, etc. To disable any of these services, deselect them under the Privacy heading.

The Content settings button includes several Chrome options, like pop-up blocking, location tracking, JavaScript settings, automatic downloads and more. Most of these settings include a Manage exceptions button. As you surf the web, Chrome will ask you if you'd like to make these exceptions. For example, when Chrome blocks a pop-up, it will notify you of the action and then ask if you'd like to allow pop-ups once or always for that site. You can then revoke those exceptions later if you need to in Content Settings.

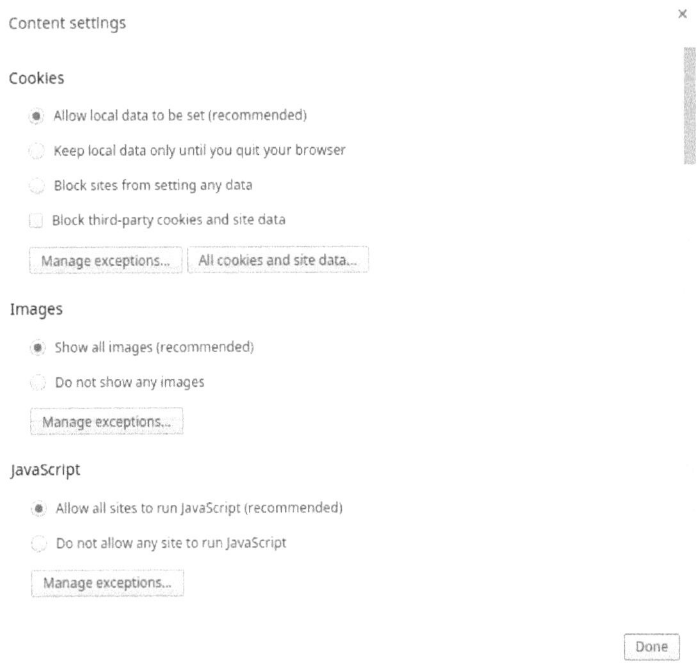

Generally, I recommend leaving these settings with their defaults, as I think there's a good balance between end-user protection and convenience of use. Nevertheless, you may occasionally need to turn off the pop-up blocker or adjust another one of these settings, and it's good to know where to find them.

WEB CONTENT

The web content settings allow you to change the default font size and page zoom for web pages. You can also choose what sort of font you'd like Chrome to display as a default.

LANGUAGES

The Languages heading allows you to turn automatic translation offers on and off. You can also manage the languages you'd like to use with Chromebook by clicking the Language and input settings button. You can add more than one by clicking the Add button in the lower left corner. The language at the top of your list will be your default language, but adding additional languages gives you the ability to set up keyboard input options so that you can quickly switch languages as needed.

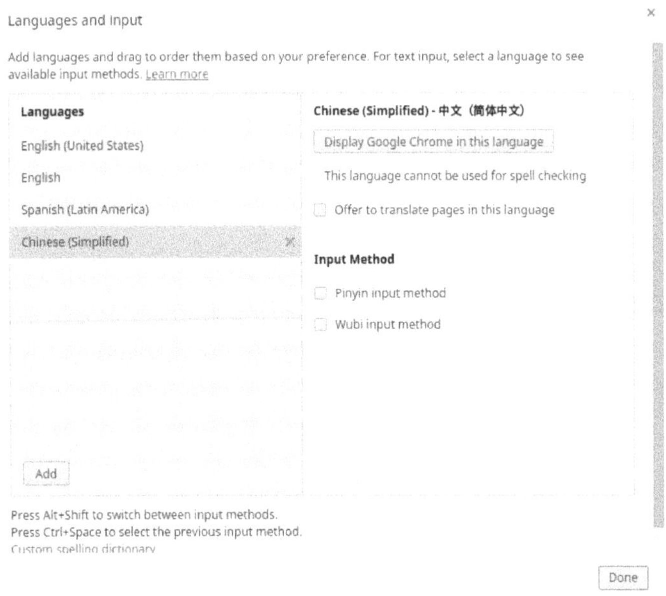

DOWNLOADS

Here you can change the way your Chromebook handles downloads. Perhaps the most useful feature here is the ability to change the default downloads location to something more accessible than the Downloads folder. Or, if you prefer, you can tell Chrome that you want it to always ask you where you want to save downloads. You can disable Google Drive here as well, though I don't recommend it.

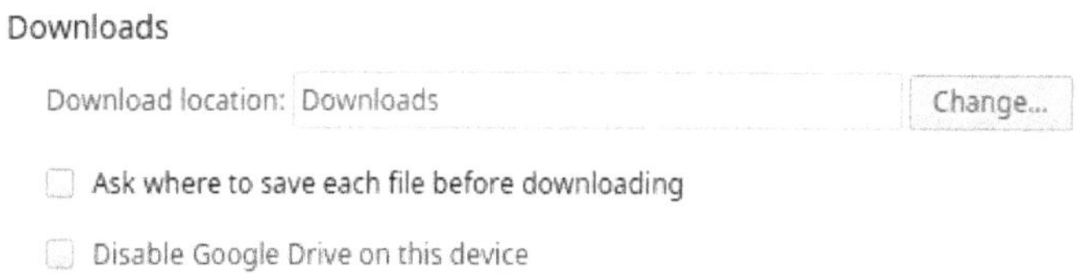

HTTPS/SSL CERTIFICATES

This area of your settings allows you to view and manage security certificates stored on your computer. The average user won't have too many reasons to make changes here, but it's good to know it's there if you're ever prompted to install or uninstall a certificate.

GOOGLE CLOUD PRINT

Google Cloud Print is Google's printing service. It allows users to send a print job over the web to their printer, rather than the traditional methods of wired or wireless printer connections. To use it, you'll need to connect your printer to your Google Cloud Print account. You'll find instructions and more information about this by clicking Learn more under the Google Cloud Print heading.

STARTUP

The On Startup heading tells Chrome what to do the first time you open it. You can start with a new tab page, or open the pages that you had open during your last use (the default option). You can also set a page or group of pages that you'd like to open. This is a great way to open your email, Facebook, the news, and your favorite blog without having to do anything but start Google Chrome.

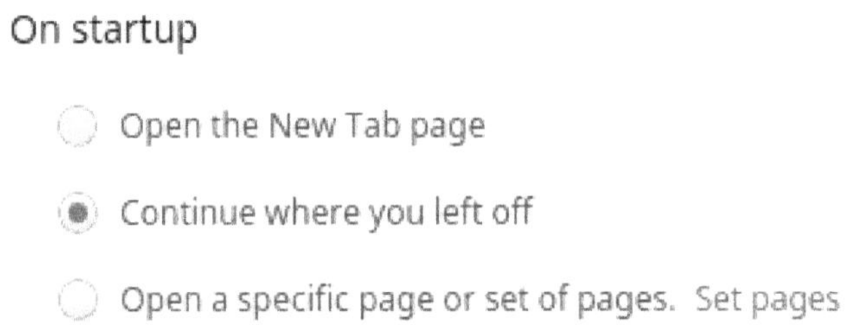

ACCESSIBILITY

The accessibility heading provides a suite of features designed to make Chromebook more accessible for individuals with impaired vision or certain motor disabilities. Select as many as you like to make your Chromebook experience more comfortable for you.

There is an additional collection of accessibility apps and extensions in the Web Store as well. To view them, click Add additional accessibility features.

POWERWASH AND RESET

The powerwash and reset options are located at the very bottom of the advanced settings screen. Powerwash is the panic button. This extreme step will completely erase everything on your Chromebook and restore it to factory settings. It can be used as an absolutely last-ditch troubleshooting measure, but just remember that it's permanent—there's no recovering from a Powerwash (though of course you can re-download anything you've purchased through Google, and since almost everything on Chromebook is a web app, you won't lose any of your files stored in Google Drive). Powerwash is also the thing to do if you're selling or giving away your Chromebook.

A less drastic approach is the Reset button. This doesn't wipe your device, but it does restore all system settings to their original defaults. If you've played with your configuration and decided you prefer the original, just hit Reset to get back to square one without losing your apps or data.

SUPERVISED ACCOUNTS

If you have any children in your house, you may want to set up supervised accounts for them. This will allow them to use your Chromebook, but with a few restrictions designed to keep them safe and you sane. You can restrict web pages and content for supervised users, and you can log in anytime to chrome.com/manage to monitor the account.

To add a supervised user, click Add user on the sign-in screen. A sign-in box will appear. Click Create a supervised user (in blue) on the right side of the box to get started.

Next, you'll name the account and set a password and profile picture. Supervised users aren't Google account users, so there's no need to set up a unique username. You can also set a password that's easy to remember, since it's for a local account instead of an online one.

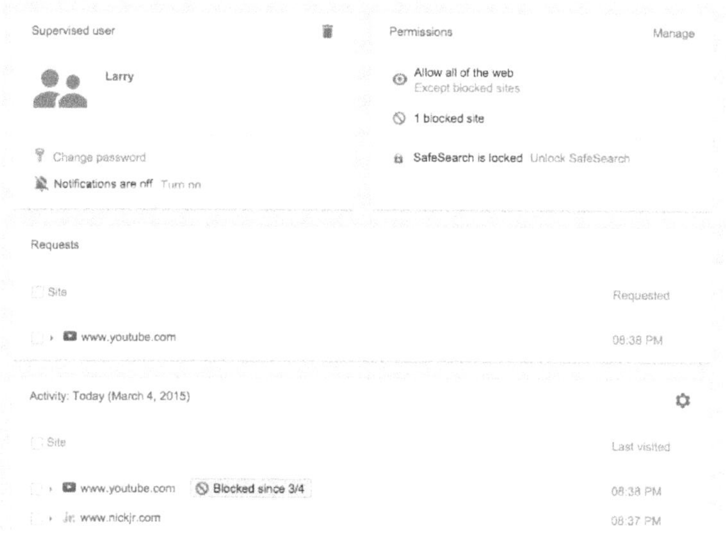

At chrome.com/manage, you can change the supervised user's password, set restricted sites, and deal with requests to unblock sites from the user, as seen above.

TROUBLESHOOTING AND MAINTAINING YOUR CHROMEBOOK

One of the best things about Chromebook is its simplicity—unlike more complex operating system software like Windows or Mac OSX, there's really very little that can go wrong. However, things can and do happen sometimes, and I'll walk you through some quick and easy troubleshooting methods here.

Check Your Battery

Also known as the "is it plugged in?" step, this is a frequent culprit in Chromebook problems. Check to be sure that your charger is connected and plugged in before you jump to any conclusions as to why your Chromebook won't wake up.

Restart

When in doubt, reboot. This often is all it takes to fix frozen systems or other irritating problems. Thanks to most Chrome apps' constant background saving processes, you rarely need to worry about losing work when you do this.

If you're having problems with an app, you can always try closing it and reopening it. If that doesn't work, you may want to try removing it from your device and then re-downloading it from the Web Store.

Getting Help and Contacting Support

If you're stuck with a Chromebook problem, try the Get Help app. It's a searchable tour of your Chromebook's features and may provide the answer you need. If that doesn't work, you might try the Google user forums at https://support.google.com/chromebook-central. Here you'll find frequently asked questions, user forums where you can search for other people with your issue (or post it yourself), and more. You'll find power Google users to be a pretty informed bunch, and the forums are an excellent resource when you run into trouble.

To get official support for your Chromebook, you can either request a call or start a chat session with a Google technician. To do this, visit support.google.com/Chromebook and click Contact Us in the top right corner.

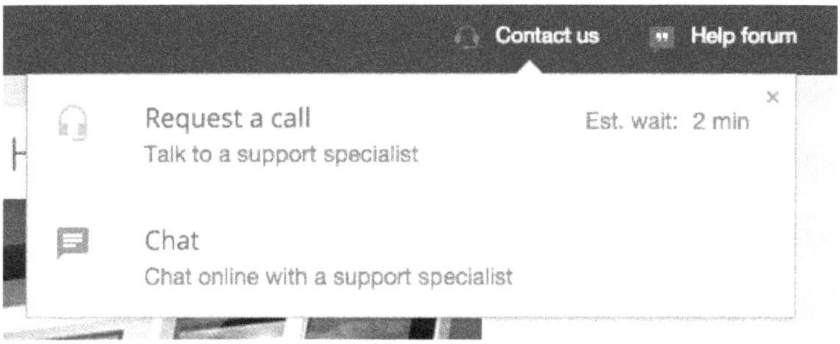

Updating Your Chromebook

Chromebook keeps itself up to date for the most part, so the only thing you need to do is be sure that it's regularly online and in use. Chrome will take care of the rest! If you ever need to see what version of Chrome you're running, you can do so by visiting Chrome Settings. Then click About Chrome OS at the top. This will display your device's update status, as well as its current version.

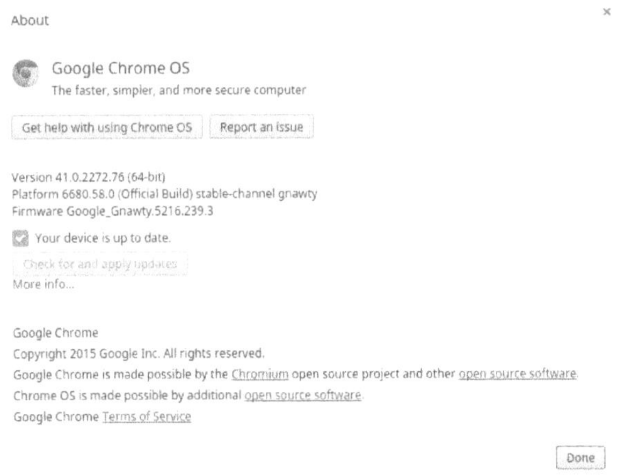

It's a good idea to periodically check that your system is updating itself. You may occasionally need to click Check for and apply updates to manually perform an update check. Sometimes new updates require a system restart, fortunately, most Chromebooks restart within seconds!

APPENDIX A: SPECS

Specification	Pixelbook	Surface Laptop	MacBook
Software	Chrome OS	Windows 10 S	macOS High Sierra
Display	12.3 inches	13.5 inches	12 inches
Resolution	2400 x 1600	2256 x 1504	2304 x 1440
Processor (base)	Intel Core i5 (seventh-gen)	Intel Core i5 (seventh-gen)	Intel Core m3 (1.2GHz, dual-core, seventh-gen)

Processor (max)	Intel Core i7 (seventh-gen)	Intel Core i7 (seventh-gen)	Intel Core i7 (1.4GHz, dual-core, seventh-gen)
RAM (base)	8GB	4GB	8GB
RAM(max)	16GB	16GB	16GB
Ports	USB-C, 3.5mm headphone jack	USB 3.0, 3.5mm headphone jack, Mini DisplayPort	USB-C, 3.5mm headphone jack
Storage	128GB, 256GB, 512GB	128GB, 256GB, 512GB, 1TB	256GB, 512GB
Weight	2.4 pounds	2.76 pounds	2.03 pounds

Starting price	$999	$999	$1,299

APPENDIX B: SHORTCUT KEYS

Popular shortcuts

- Open the Google Assistant: Press 
- Search your device, apps, web and more: Press 
- Open the status area (where your account picture appears): Press 
- Take a screenshot: Press Ctrl + 
- Take a partial screenshot: Press Ctrl + Shift + , then click and drag

- Turn Caps Lock on or off: Press Alt + Search
- Lock your screen: Press Search + L
- Sign out of your Google account: Press Ctrl + Shift + q (twice)

All other shortcuts

Note: If you're using a Windows or Mac keyboard, use the Windows key or Command key in place of the Search key.

Tabs and windows

Open a new window	Ctrl + n
Open a new window in incognito mode	Ctrl + Shift + n
Open a new tab	Ctrl + t

Open a file in the browser	Ctrl + o
Close the current tab	Ctrl + w
Close the current window	Ctrl + Shift + w
Reopen the last tab or window you closed	Ctrl + Shift + t
Go to tabs 1-8 in the window	Ctrl + 1 through Ctrl + 8
Go to the last tab in the window	Ctrl + 9
Go to the next tab in the window	Ctrl + Tab

Go to the previous tab in the window	Ctrl + Shift + Tab
Switch quickly between windows	Press & hold Alt, tap Tab until you get to the window you want to open, then release.
Open the window you used least recently	Press & hold Alt + Shift, tap Tab until you get to the window you want to open, then release.
Go to previous page in your browsing history	Alt + left arrow
Go to the next page in your browsing history	Alt + right arrow
Open the link in a new tab in the background	Press Ctrl and click a link

Open the link in a new tab and switch to the new tab	Press Ctrl + Shift and click a link
Open the link in a new window	Press Shift and click a link
Open the link in the tab	Drag the link to the tab's address bar
Open the link in a new tab	Drag the link to a blank area on the tab strip
Open the web page in a new tab	Type a web address (URL) in the address bar, then press Alt + Enter
Return the tab to its original posi-tion	While dragging the tab, press Esc

Dock a window on the left	Alt + [
Dock a window on the right	Alt +]

Page & Web Browser

Page up	Alt or Search and up arrow
Page down	Alt or Search and down arrow
Scroll down the web page	Space bar
Go to top of page	Ctrl + Alt and up arrow
Go to bottom of page	Ctrl + Alt and down arrow
Print your current page	Ctrl + p

Save your current page	Ctrl + s
Reload your current page	Ctrl + r
Reload your current page without using cached content	Ctrl + Shift + r
Zoom in on the page	Ctrl and +
Zoom out on the page	Ctrl and -
Reset zoom level	Ctrl + 0
Stop the loading of your current page	Esc
Right-click a link	Press Alt and click a link
Open the link in a new tab in the background	Press Ctrl and click a link

Save the link as a bookmark	Drag link to bookmarks bar
Save your current web page as a bookmark	Ctrl + d
Save all open pages in your current window as bookmarks in a new folder	Ctrl + Shift + d
Search the current page	Ctrl + f
Go to the next match for your search	Ctrl + g or Enter
Go to the previous match for your search	Ctrl + Shift + g or Shift + Enter
Perform a Google search	 or Ctrl + k or Ctrl + e

Add www. and .com to your input in the address bar, then open the page	Ctrl + Enter
View page source	Ctrl + u
Show or hide the Developer Tools panel	Ctrl + Shift + i
Show or hide the DOM Inspector	Ctrl + Shift + j
Show or hide the bookmarks bar	Ctrl + Shift + b
Open the History page	Ctrl + h
Open the Downloads page	Ctrl + j

System & Display Settings

Open the Files app	Alt + Shift + m

Preview a file in the Files app	Select the file, then press Space
Display hidden files in the Files app	Ctrl + .
Open the status area (where your account picture appears)	 or Shift + Alt + s
Click icons 1-8 on your shelf	Alt + 1 through Alt + 8
Click the last icon on your shelf	Alt + 9
Use F keys (F1 to F12)	Search + 1 through Search + =
See your notifications	Alt + Shift + n

Change screen resolution	Ctrl + Shift and + or -
Reset screen resolution to default	Ctrl + Shift + 0
Rotate screen 90 degrees	Ctrl + Shift + 
Switch to the next user	Ctrl + Alt + .
Switch to the previous user	Ctrl + Alt + ,

Text Editing

Turn Caps Lock on or off	Alt + Search
Select everything on the page	Ctrl + a
Select the content in the address bar	Ctrl + L or Alt + d

Select the next word or letter	Ctrl + Shift and right arrow
Select text to the end of the line	Shift + Search and right arrow
Select text to the beginning of the line	Shift + Search and left arrow
Select previous word or letter	Ctrl + Shift and left arrow
Move to the end of the next word	Ctrl and right arrow
Move to the start of the previous word	Ctrl and left arrow
Go to end of document	Ctrl + Search and right arrow

Go to beginning of document	Ctrl + Search and left arrow
Copy selected content to the clipboard	Ctrl + c
Paste content from the clip-board	Ctrl + v
Paste content from the clip-board as plain text	Ctrl + Shift + v
Cut	Ctrl + x
Delete the previous word	Ctrl + Back-space
Delete the next letter (forward delete)	Alt + Back-space
Undo your last action	Ctrl + z

Redo your last action	Ctrl + Shift + z
Switch between the keyboard languages you've set. Learn how to choose your keyboard language.	Ctrl + Shift + Space
Switch to the previous keyboard language you were using. Learn how to choose your keyboard language.	Ctrl + Space
Dim keyboard (for backlit keyboards only)	Alt + 
Make keyboard brighter (for backlit keyboards only)	Alt + 

Accessibility

Learn how to make your Pixelbook accessible.

Turn ChromeVox (spoken feedback) on or off	Ctrl + Alt + z

Turn on high contrast mode	Ctrl + Search + h
Highlight the launcher button on your shelf	Shift + Alt + L
Highlight the next item on your shelf	Shift + Alt + L, then Tab or right arrow
Highlight the previous item on your shelf	Shift + Alt + L, then Shift + Tab or left arrow
Open the highlighted button on your shelf	Shift + Alt + L, then Space or Enter
Remove the highlight from a button on your shelf	Shift + Alt + L, then Esc
Switch focus between:	Ctrl + ←

• Status area (where your account picture appears) • Launcher • Address bar • Bookmarks bar (if visible) • The web page that's open • Downloads bar (if visible)	
Highlight the bookmarks bar (if shown)	Alt + Shift + b
Highlight the row with the address bar	Shift + Alt + t
Open right-click menu for highlighted item	Shift + 

About the Author

Scott La Counte is a librarian and writer. His first book, *Queit, Please: Dispatches from a Public Librarian* (Da Capo 2008) was the editor's choice for the Chicago Tribune and a Discovery title for the Los Angeles Times; in 2011, he published the YA book The N00b Warriors, which became a #1 Amazon bestseller; his most recent book is *#OrganicJesus: Finding Your Way to an Unprocessed, GMO-Free Christianity* (Kregel 2016).

He has written dozens of best-selling how-to guides on tech products.

You can connect with him at ScottDouglas.org.

www.ingramcontent.com/pod-product-compliance
Ingram Content Group UK Ltd.
Pitfield, Milton Keynes, MK11 3LW, UK
UKHW040634210425
5545UKWH00028B/180

9 781629 176079